S. C Alexander

The Stone Kingdom

Or, the United States and America as Seen by the Prophets

S. C Alexander

The Stone Kingdom
Or, the United States and America as Seen by the Prophets

ISBN/EAN: 9783337100889

Printed in Europe, USA, Canada, Australia, Japan

Cover: Foto ©Lupo / pixelio.de

More available books at **www.hansebooks.com**

THE STONE KINGDOM

OR THE

UNITED STATES AND AMERICA

AS SEEN BY THE PROPHETS.

BY

REV. S. C. ÁLEXANDER, A. M.

WE HAVE WRITTEN ONLY ON THE FULFILLED.

" Blessed is he that readeth, and they that hear the words of this prophecy,
and keep those things which are written therein : for the
time is at hand."—*Rev. i. 3.*

———◄•►———

ST. LOUIS:
FARRIS, SMITH & CO. PRINT.
1885.

DEDICATED

PREFACE.

This little work is sent out in behalf of the Inspiration of the Bible. Infidels try to avoid the point of the argument, drawn from the fulfillment of ancient prophecies about Babylon, Jerusalem, Egypt, and scores of others, by saying they were " fixed-up jobs," away back in the ages, to support the claims of Christianity. But here, in our own America, is a great country, more than 2500 years removed from the writers of prophecy, which has filled, and is now filling the prophetic programme with astonishing exactness in numberless particulars, even as the shadow fits the substance.

This country, so far removed from the prophets, furnishes no possible chance for collusion or deception. Prophecy tells us why this country was not discovered before it was —" Surely the isles shall wait for me ; " and the " undiscovered lands in the Atlantic " waited till the set time. Prophecy tells us what nation should discover this land, and open the way for immigration. " The ships of Tarshish—or Spain—shall be first to bring thy sons from afar." And it was so. The time of the setting up of the United States government was accurately given, and it was set up on the very day mentioned by the prophets. Prophecy tells us that this government should be set up in thirteen States. And it was so. Prophecy tells us that these States should " extend from the sea on the east to the great sea on the west." And it is so. Prophecy tells us that this " Stone shall fill the whole earth." And is it not accomplishing this prophecy most wonderfully, by giving civil and religious liberty to the nations.

The example of our country is a living, eloquent herald, proclaiming to the peoples, what they may be, and what they ought to be—*free men*—free from the bondage of monarchs, hierarchs, and despots ; and are not the nations hearing, heeding, moving ? The peoples long oppressed are now clamoring for their rights as men. The example of our providential government, the growth and prosperity of the " Stone " is the disturbing cause of unrest among the autocracies and kingdoms of earth. As a demonstration of this truth, every crowned head in Europe is a prisoner to-day in his own palace. These royalties are afraid of the people : and well they may be, for it is written, " The thrones shall be cast down."

In confirmation of these truths, we quote the opinion of John Bright, England's great Commoner, July 2, 1885 : " The real interests of the masses are trodden under foot, in deference to false notions of glory and national honor. I cannot help thinking that Europe is marching towards some great catastrophe of crushing weight. The military system cannot indefinitely be supported with patience ; and the population, driven to despair, may possibly before long sweep away the royalties and pretended statesmen who govern in their names."

Then go little work, and tell the people that the God of prophecy is the God of providence. Tell them that His plans reach through all time, and through all countries, and that they are daily being realized in the ceaseless march of His providences. And by this little volume may the people see more clearly than ever, that "the Lord God Omnipotent reigneth," and "doeth according to His will in the army of heaven, and among the inhabitants of the earth; and none can stay His hand, or say unto Him, 'What doest thou?'"

CONTENTS.

IX

CHAPTER X.

"THE WAITING ISLES,"

Or our Country Described by the Prophet.—Isaiah lx........ 160

CHAPTER XI.

"BEHOLD I DO A NEW THING,"

Or the Primal Curse Rolling Back.—Isaiah xliii: 18–21...... 194

CHAPTER XII.

THE STONE KINGDOM A POLITICAL POWER.

"SHALL NEVER DESTROY ITSELF."

Confirmed by one of the endings of the 42 months, which points with exactness to May 26th, A. D. 1865, when the last of the Confederate forces were surrendered............ 207

CHAPTER XIII.

OUR COUNTRY AFTER THE PROPHETIC PATTERN.

And what our Rulers "Ought to do."..... 217

CHAPTER I.

INTRODUCTION.

"The Scriptures must be fulfilled."

IN the study of the prophecies, there are certain great principles that ought to be adhered to with the sacredness of a divine injunction.

1st. Students of God's word should sit as children at the *Master's* feet, willing and anxious to be taught, but never attempt to teach the Master. This would be unpardonable presumption and impudence. To search the Scriptures and to find out what the Lord has said, is the duty and legitimate work of the student. "Blessed is he that readeth and they that hear the words of this prophecy and keep those things which are written therein; for the time is at hand."

2nd. We should never study the Word with *preconceived* notions as to what the

13

Lord ought to have said. We should never make up a verdict, and then try to prove its justness from a part of the testimony. But first hear all the testimony of *prophecy and providence*, and then righteously make up the verdict as the result of such testimony.

3rd. The testimony of God's Word should never be *ignored*, or *twisted* from its true intent. Either of these would be a great wrong and thereby "darken counsel by words without knowledge."

4th. *Human precedents*, however numerous, great or learned, should never be quoted as correct or authoritative against a direct "Thus saith the Lord." In other words, old ruts through the swamps of error should not be followed, simply because they are old, when the Lord hath opened " a new and living way which He hath consecrated for us."

5th. In order to a correct interpretation of Old Testament prophecies, a radical examination of the Hebrew words is absolutely necessary, in order to get the meaning of the Spirit. And generally I have found the main root, or principal meaning of the word, the one that expresses the true sense of the prophecy. Very rarely a tropical meaning is selected, unless it be in some minute detail.

Observation 1st. I rise from these studies thoroughly confirmed in the belief of the *ipsissima verba* theory of inspiration. For the prophets wrote about and described things which they never saw realized, and about things scores and thousands of years ahead of them, with astonishing exactness. This would have been utterly impossible, had the Lord not told them the *words* to write and speak. The Bible is made up of the words of God ; man only wrote them down or delivered them, but the Spirit told His prophets what to write. The Lord made the vision pass before the prophet, then He told him how to tell the vision. This truth is demonstrated in the fulfillment of every prophecy. The astonishing fitness of every word in the prophetic description as is manifested in the fulfillment, is evidence of the divine origin of the words. Especially is this fact exhibited in some of those prophecies written 2,500 years ago, and now fulfilled before our eyes with amazing exactness. This is demonstration that the Bible is God's Word.

Observation 2nd. We do not ask scholars to accept our interpretation of these prophecies as correct, until they are satisfied of their truthfulness. But we do most solemnly protest against the publication or expression of adverse opinions, until they also have prayerfully and carefully examined every word of these prophecies in the inspired original: then if they can "show unto you a more excellent way," or a more truthful and consistent interpretation of these prophecies fulfilled, such a showing will be gratefully received.

Observation 3rd. The prophecies treated upon in this book, have been fulfilled, or are now in the process of fulfillment. We have scrupulously avoided speculations on the unrealized. Our aim is to speak of that part of the divine programme which is now history and past; and also of that part which is now passing.

SOURCES OF INFORMATION.

We have obtained valuable suggestions from Addison Alexander, from Lowth on the prophecies, from Thomas Scott. One suggestion from Sir Isaac Newton gave encouragement, and threw light over the whole field. Many hints from S. D. Baldwin, an independent and original thinker, have been valuable. In fact, he was a great man, but he "dealt too much in futures" and failed. His discovery of the "key" to "the times" of the prophets, in the word *hathak*, "to cut off," "to abbreviate," is absolutely wonderful, when applied to prophecies fulfilled, where he has history to guide him. But his "key" utterly fails in the unfulfilled, for the *lack* of a *guide.*

The great mass of commentators only furnish *negative* help, by showing the unfitness and unsatisfactoriness of their expositions of these prophecies which lead the mind to seek for "a better way." But by far the greatest help is obtained from a critical examination of the inspired words in the original. From them, volumes of information and floods of light burst upon the astonished mind. The student there beholds the grandeur of truth as he never saw it before. Also like other students, I have kept my eyes open and tried to pick up information wherever I could find it.

CHAPTER II.

THE IMAGE OF MONARCHY.

"The Stone cut out of the Mountain" and its Mission.—*Dan. ii.**

THE novelty of our subject naturally tends to awaken incredulity and to arouse opposition. Any departure from the beaten track of centuries must be fortified with truth and armed with demonstration, or fall ingloriously before the terrible onset. Pride of opinion, and especially religious opinions, hoary with age, will muster all their forces for the fray both real and imaginary. Reason and learning will whet their swords and burnish their armor for the conflict. But *truth* all

---

* The principal part of chapters II., III. and IV., was first written and delivered as a Lecture on the "Stone Kingdom." This was subsequently enlarged into this little volume. Its size coul l easily have been doubled, but the writer desired only to unfold a few of those great and unmistakable pictures of our country, to point to the gold "cropping out" on the surface, and thereby direct the Bible student to rich veins of unexpected truth.

18

alone, like the son of Jesse, conscious of his
strength, moves forward with unfaltering step
and hurls with deadly aim the stones gathered
from the brook of revelation, at giant error,
till he who had defied the armies of Israel and
hindered his progress, lies dead at his feet.
Ridicule and sophistry, clothed in the worn-
out garments of the cast-off tawdry of sages,
will combine to laugh at and to overthrow
that which history, facts and argument never
will attempt. This much we expect. But all
we ask is a candid hearing of the testimony,
before your verdict is rendered. We ask you
to listen to facts, not theory—to truth not
fanaticism—to the testimony of divinely appointed witnesses. Then, for these reasons, I
demand that you hear me for my cause.

There is a divine reason assigned why these
prophecies were not correctly interpreted at
an earlier period. When Daniel asked earn-
estly to find out more about the revealed programme of the nations, the Lord said: "Go
thy way, Daniel, for the words are closed up
and sealed till the time of the end." Hence
all those wonderful prophecies relating to the
United States, were not only closed up, but

sealed, and that seal could not be broken by
human astuteness or wisdom, until the time
specified, a period called "the time of the
end." Then the God of prophecy and providence will Himself break the seal and open
the book. That period of "the time of the
end" has arrived. The divine testimony of
this fact is, that "many shall run to and fro,
and knowledge shall be increased." This is
the inscription, written on a mile-post let
down from heaven and set up on the great
highway of prophecy, to show pilgrims where
they are, as they wend their way along the
track of time, and to tell them how far they
are on their journey. Was there ever such a
running to and fro since the world was made,
or such an increase in knowledge as now is?
By this we know that the period of "the time
of the end" has arrived, and that the seal has
been broken, and the book has been opened,
so that, he that runneth may read. That
which once was profound darkness to the
great and learned, may now be as clear as
noonday to children in the Scriptures.

Another reason why these wonderful prophecies have always been wrongly interpreted,

and a false and forced application given them,
is because all the old standard and accepted
commentators, venerable names, were Euro-
peans. They would place one leg of the com
pass of prophecy in their own land, and with
the other sweep round the horizon of the old
world, and leave America—one-third of the
earth's surface—entirely outside. Their map
of prophecy is very much like a Chinese map
of the world, in which the Celestial Empire
occupies the whole space, except two little
spots away up in the northwest corner about
the size of a dime, to represent Europe and
America, and these are called " Barbarian
Isles."

The eternal plans of the Great God extend
from eternity to eternity, and embrace all time
and all things. Is it probable, therefore, is it
reasonable that our great country, with its
teeming magnificence — now the dread and
glory of all lands—should have no place in
the divine prophecies? Is it probable, is it
reasonable that our country, with its scores of
millions of immortals, and room for untold
millions more, where mind is making its
grandest triumphs over matter, where eternal

truth, and the Church of the Lord Jesus Christ
are gaining unprecedented victories, where
civil and religious liberty flourish unre-
strained, where time's noblest offspring brings
her choicest gifts into the temple of God—is it
reasonable that this land should have no place
in the divine programme of nations, when
Edom and Moab and Tyre and Sidon, and
scores of other places, but mere specks on the
earth, whose prophecies now fulfilled are their
histories? Yes, our country now performing,
and yet destined to perform, so glorious a part
in the drama of nations, has its full share assigned it, as we shall presently see.

The first prophecy which we invite you to
consider, as foretelling the rise and mission
of our country, is the *fifth government*, or the
"Stone Kingdom" of Daniel, 2nd chapter.
The Bible student will remember that the term
"kingdom" in the prophecies, is a convertible
term with *government*. In the dream of Nebuchadnezzar, he saw a great image whose brightness was excellent, and the form thereof was
terrible. It represented all of monarchy from
that time henceforth. "This image's head
was of fine gold, his breast and his arms were

of silver, his belly and thighs of brass, his
legs of iron, his feet part of iron and part of
clay. Thou sawest till that a stone was cut
out without hands, which smote the image
upon his feet, that were of iron and clay, and
brake them to pieces." The interpretation
of this dream is, Thou, O King, art this head
of gold, in whom the Babylonian Empire culminated. The two arms and breast of silver
represented the Medo-Persian Empire which
culminated in Cyrus. The belly and thighs
of brass represented the Macedonian Empire,
which culminated in the reign of Alexander
the Great. The legs of iron represent the
Roman Empire, which stood for 1,000 years,
on the legs of her trained legions, and culminated in the twelve Cæsars. Thus far there
is no dispute. European and American expositors all agree in this interpretation. The
fulfillment perfectly coincides with prophecy.
The terrible programme thus far has been fully
enacted, amid the crash of Empires, and the
groans of millions. "And whereas thou sawest the feet and toes, part of potter's clay and
part of iron, the kingdom shall be divided,
but there shall be in it of the strength of

the iron, forasmuch as thou sawest the iron
mixed with miry clay. And as the toes of
the feet were part of iron and part of clay, so
the kingdom shall be partly strong and partly
broken." The feet and toe governments were
formed out of the territory which the legs of
iron, or Roman Empire, stood upon. And as
the toes grew out, a new element of weakness
was incorporated with them—iron mixed with
miry clay. So that their governments were
partly strong and partly broken. This we
think forcefully represents the Union of Church
and State. As there can be no chemical amalgam between clay and iron, so there never has
been, and never can be, any happy and prosperous union between Church and State.
" Whereas thou sawest iron mixed with miry
clay—*they* shall mingle themselves with the
seed of men—but they shall not cleave one
to another, even as iron is not mixed with
clay." Here we have a plain statement that
a superior order of men, will join an inferior
order—or the Church shall be joined to the
State. Such a government must, from its want
of cohesion, from lack of affinity between its
parts, and great dissimilarity, from its per-

version of the ends of one, and the prosti-
tution of the aims of the other, always be
partly strong and partly broken, a politico-
ecclesiastical concubinage that would curse
the nations of the earth. These toe govern-ᵥ
ments and their successors, as represented in
the image of Nebuchadnezzar, have stood for
many centuries, and are still standing in the
territory of monarchy and absolutism, and
still continue the illegitimate and unnatural
union of iron and miry clay, still cramping
freedom of thought and the progress of truth,
and still hindering the growth of civil and
religious liberty. Such is the image of monarchy, and its interpretation.

It is necessary to the proper understanding
of the fifth government or Stone Kingdom and
its great mission, to read what saith the Lord.
Dan. ii : 34, 35. "Thou sawest till that a
stone was cut out without hands, which smote
the image upon his feet, that were of iron and
clay, and brake them to pieces. Then was
the iron, the clay, the brass, the silver and the
gold broken to pieces together, and became
like the chaff of the summer threshing-floors,
and the wind carried them away, that no place

was found for them. And the stone that smote the image became a great mountain and filled the whole earth." The interpretation of this sublime symbol was revealed to Daniel, chap. ii:44,45. "And in the days of these kings, shall the God of heaven set up a kingdom, which shall never be destroyed, and the kingdom shall not be left to other people, but it shall break in pieces, and consume all these kingdoms, and it shall stand forever. Forasmuch as thou sawest that the stone was cut out of the mountain without hands, and that it brake in pieces the iron, the brass, the clay, the silver and the gold, the great God hath made known to the king what shall come to pass hereafter; and the dream is certain, and the interpretation thereof sure."

"In the days of these kings, shall the God of heaven set up a kingdom." What kingdom has the God of heaven set up? Almost all European commentators say it was the setting up of Christianity. But this cannot be the meaning of the prophet, for four reasons: 1st. Because the kingdom or government to be set up, was to be set up "in the days of these kings"—these ten-toe kings.

But Christianity was set up in the reign of *one* king—*one* Augustus Cæsar. Therefore this old interpretation will not fit the *time*, and of course cannot be true.   2nd. The Stone Kingdom did not rise in the proper *place* for Christianity.   Jesus was born in Bethlehem of Judea, at that time a Roman province. But the Stone Kingdom was to be set up entirely outside of the Roman Empire, and outside of all her subsequent ten-toe kingdoms.   It was to strike from without, upon the image of monarchy.   It was to be hurled with mighty force against the feet of the image and crush it to atoms, so that it would fly like chaff before the winds of the summer threshing floors.   3rd. The Stone Kingdom could not have been set up at the time Christianity arose, for then the Romans claimed all the known world: "There went out a decree from Cæsar Augustus, that all the world should be taxed."   But there was a land, my countrymen, "where the Roman cohorts were never marshalled."   A land which the God of providence had concealed from Rome's cupidity and her conquering armies.   That land is our own America.   The

only portion of the globe that suits, in every
repect, the rise of the promised, *great nationality*, that fully meets the geography, place,
and time of the fifth kingdom which the God
of heaven would " set up." 4th. The kingdom of Christ is a *spiritual* power, and con-
quers by *love*. But the Stone Kingdom was
to be clothed with great political and military
power, and the enginery of battle, to crush,
to destroy, and to break to pieces the nations
of earth that oppose its progress. For this
and all these reasons, it is perfectly clear
that Christianity is not, and cannot be, the
Stone Kingdom.

But this fifth government is to be a great
Christian Republic, where Church and State
are each independent, and yet each dependent,
where each enjoys the largest degree of
liberty consistent with conscience and right,
where the Church may put on her beautiful
garments and shine forth in all her glory,
where every man may worship God according
to the dictates of his conscience and none
dare disturb him or make him afraid. This
land, my countrymen, is yours, which God
gave to our fathers and to us.

Let us examine more definitely as to the *time* of the setting up of the Stone Kingdom. It will be, Dan. xii : 7, when " the power of the holy people," or the friends of civil and religious liberty " shall cease to be scattered," when " many shall run to and fro and knowledge shall be increased," when " the time of the end" shall come: then will the Stone Kingdom, or fifth nationality, be set up.

In Dan. xii : 7, it is said that it will be " a time. times and an half " from the taking away of the daily sacrifice, or from the burning of the Temple by the Romans under Titus, when, after 1,260 symbolic years, from this date, during which the persecuting power shall have accomplished to scatter the power of the holy people, all these things shall be finished. Now the burning of the Temple occurred, according to the most accurate calculation, on the 189th day of A. D. 68. From this date onward, 1,260 prophetic days or years will bring us to the beginning of "the time of the end," or the setting up of the Stone Kingdom. Now how to count this time accurately, or satisfactorily, has been the problem of ages. But we think the key has been discovered. The words that were closed up and sealed so long, are now opened and the seal broken. The Lord sealed up this knowledge until "the time of the end," a period that would be signalized by great locomotion and amazing increase in knowledge. Now since the time of the end has come, God in His providence, has broken the seal and given us the long hidden "key" to the times of the prophecies. This key is found in the 70 weeks of Daniel, Chap. ix. "Seventy weeks are *determined* upon thy people and upon thy holy city," etc. The word translated *determined* in Hebrew is *nechtack* from the root *hathak* which means to "cut off, to abbreviate, to shorten." Then the 70 weeks are "cut off" or abbreviated time, to which sacred time must be added, to fill out to solar time. These 70 weeks are to begin at the time Cyrus gave the commandment to restore and to build Jerusalem. This decree was published in the last month of the year 537 B. C., about December 6th, as ascertained by historic records and also by an eclipse of the sun predicted by Thales of Miletus. The crucifixion of Christ occurred on March 25, A. D. 29 (vulgar era.) This date is also ascertained by historic records, and an eclipse of the moon from which dates are reckoned. The 70 weeks have two endings, one at the crucifixion of Messiah, and the other at the burning of the Temple and destruction of Jerusalem.

Let us see how this calculation is made. The 70 weeks are 70 weeks of years, or 490 years. Add one-seventh for sabbatic time, and we have 560 symbolic years of 360 parts. And since a symbolic year may stand for any Hebrew year of years, it may stand for one of 364 parts. Then we have the equation $360: 364 :: 560 : 566\frac{2}{9}$ years composed of 364 days each. Now, reduce this to solar time of 365 days, 5 hours, 48 minutes and $47\frac{1}{10}$ seconds; and we have exactly 564 years and 109 days, as the fulfillment of the prophecy shows, from the decree of Cyrus " to restore and build Jerusalem " to the crucifixion of Christ. The other ending, is to be at the burning of the Temple and the taking away of the daily sacrifice. This may be found by several different calculations, but one is sufficient, and is as follows. Forty-two weeks may represent an abbreviated Hebrew year of 364 parts.

Then we have the following equation 42: 364 :: 70 : 606⅔. The text gives no intimation of what kind of a year the 70 weeks were to be realized in. That only can be determined by the fulfillment. Then as 366 days make the longest year, we will try it and see. By reducing the 606⅔ symbolic years, to solar time, we have the following: 366:364:: 606⅔=603 years and 129 days—the exact solar time from the decree of Cyrus to the burning of the Temple, and taking away of the daily sacrifice. A part of a Hebrew day is taken for a whole.

Having found the key by which to solve the "time, times and an half," or the 1,260 days— the length of time that lies between the burning of the Temple and the setting up of the Stone Kingdom, we proceed, thus: 3½ times is equal to 1,260 symbolic years: to this we add ⅐ or sabbatic time, which is equal to 1,440: again, add to this result Sabbath day time or ⅙, and we have 1,680. Now, since 360 may represent any Hebrew year, it may represent the year of 366 days, then we have the equation 360: 366::1,680=1,708 years or 623,833 days,

which, added to the 189th day of the year
A. D. 68, when the Temple was burned, brings
us down exactly to July 4, 1776, when "a
nation was born in a day," when the Stone
Kingdom was set up, when our own great
nationality began, when the United States
declared themselves independent, threw off
the yoke of tyranny, and put absolutism
under foot. This marks the beginning of
"the time of the end," when civil and religious liberty would begin their growth, to bless
the crushed millions of earth. These figures
are astonishing. These facts are startling,
and the truths brought out are grandly sublime. As the four great empires, represented
in the image of monarchy, must be succeeded
by a fifth government, entirely different in
character, and as the United States of
America is the only great nation that ever has
risen, or ever can rise, to fill the great mission
of the fifth government as to *time, geography,*
and character, we are forced to the inevitable
conclusion that our glorious Christian Republic is the Stone Kingdom that "the God of
heaven should set up."

Bishop Berkeley, of Ireland, about 200 years ago, seemed to catch a glimpse of the coming kingdom, when he wrote—

" Westward the star of empire makes its way :
    The first four acts are already past,
The fifth shall close the drama with the day ;
Time's noblest offspring is the last."

Next, observe that the Stone "smote the image upon his feet," Dan. ii: 34. And "the kingdom shall be divided." "And as the toes of the feet were part of iron and part of clay," there could be no possible amalgam between the iron and the clay. "*They* shall mingle themselves with the seed of men." A higher order of men shall be joined to an inferior order. In other words, the Church shall be joined to the State. "But they shall not cleave one to another, even as iron is not mixed with clay." It is upon this divided part, or upon the ten-toe kingdoms of Church and State, which is "partly strong and partly broken," that the Stone is to strike with crushing effect. The chief mission of this great fifth nationality, is the utter destruction of Church and State union, as well as all ecclesiastical and political despotism, from the face of the earth. Does not the constitution of our government forever separate between Church and State? And however much our people may be divided on political matters, they are unanimously and forever opposed to Church and State union. And does not the whole genius, history and character of our people exactly meet the requirements and character of the Stone Kingdom? The chronology of our government exactly synchronizes with the Stone, Dan. ii: 44. "In the days of these kings" of the ten-toe kingdoms, "the God of heaven shall set up a kingdom" or government. Our own United States, and no other nation on earth, was set up in the *time specified*, and capable of doing the work assigned to the Stone Government which was cut out of the mountain of Christianity.

CHAPTER III.

A SYMBOL OF THE UNITED STATES.

The Man-Child of the Winged Woman.—Rev. xii.

IN order to confirm the wonderful truths in the preceding chapter, let us examine and see how astonishingly the Man-Child of the winged woman in the wilderness, symbolizes the United States.

Rev. xii: "And there appeared a great wonder in heaven, a woman clothed with the sun and the moon under her feet, and upon her head a crown of twelve stars. And she being with child cried, travailing in birth and pained to be delivered. And there appeared another wonder in heaven, and behold, a great red dragon having seven heads and ten horns and seven crowns upon his heads. . . . . . And the dragon stood before the woman, which was ready to be delivered, to devour her child, as soon as it

36

was born. And she brought forth a MAN-
CHILD who was to rule all nations with a rod
of iron, and her child was caught up unto
God and to His throne. . . . And to the
woman were given two wings of a great eagle
that she might fly into the wilderness into
her place; where she is nourished for a *time*
and *times* and *half a time* from the face of
the serpent. And the serpent cast out of his
mouth water as a flood after the woman, that
he might cause her to be carried away of the
flood; and the earth helped the woman and
the earth opened her mouth and swallowed
up the flood which the dragon cast out of his
mouth, and the dragon was wroth with the
woman," etc. It is generally agreed that the
Church of Christ is represented by the woman
in this symbol. And the Man-Child is the
offspring of the Church, and symbolizes a
great Christian nationality that was to be a
child of the wonderful providence of Almighty
God, to whom an iron rod was given to rule
all nations. Here we are reminded of the
crushing of the stone. Ruling with "a rod
of iron," is emblematic of great political
power.

The birth of the Man-Child after long travail and distressing pains, most graphically represents the birth of the United States. This interpretation seems to accord with the prophecy of Isaiah. "Before she travailed, she brought forth, before her pain came she was delivered of a Man-Child. Who hath heard such things? Who hath seen such things? Shall the earth be made to bring forth in one day? Or shall a nation be born at once? for as soon as Zion travailed she brought forth." The term "Zion" means the Church of God, and fixes the symbolic meaning of the "woman clothed with the sun." And the Man-Child is in apposition to "a nation born at once." Does not this wonderful symbol in Revelation most graphically foreshadow the rise of our nationality? 1st. The Man-Child was the offspring of enlightened religion. 2nd. Its destruction was determined upon by the great red dragon of despotism. 3rd. A "rod of iron" or political authority was given to the Man-Child to rule. 4th. The Man-Child and his mother were helped by the "earth" (that part of the earth covered by the old Roman Empire is called in

prophecy the " *Earth*") when floods of armies were ready to sweep the Man-Child into
destruction. The " earth," or that part of the
old Roman Empire, now occupied by Spain
and Holland, wanged war with Egland, at the
time of the birth of the Man-Child, and swallowed up much of the flood of the armies and
thereby helped the woman. While France
came directly to our assistance, and Russia
declared neutrality. Thus in various ways
the " earth " helped the woman, and the Man-
Child was rescued. 5th. " The Child was
caught up to the throne of God," means that
the wonderful providence of God was manifested towards our new-born nation—almost
without arms, without resources, without
money. The God of providence and the God
of battles gave us the victory. Truly the
God of Washington was on our side, and the
Man-Child or the United States was not
destroyed, but now lives to bless the nations
of earth. It opens a wide door for and wel-
comes the oppressed of all lands to a home of
civil and religious liberty. The coincidences
between the Man-Child and the rise of the
United States are so numerous and so won-

derfully accurate, that the conclusion is a forceful demonstration.

This "great wonder" that John saw, is almost a photographic likeness of the Church and our country.

1st. The "sun" is a symbol of civil government, exercising superior power. See Gen. xxxvii : 9; Ps. lxxxix : 36; Isa. lx : 20; Jer. xv : 9; etc. So does the government of the United States exercise a superior or controlling power over the States.

2nd. The "twelve stars" also represent governments shining in connection with the sun. Notice here the striking likeness of the symbol that there were "twelve patriarchs," and twelve Jewish tribes often called "the twelve tribes of Israel." But every one knows there were thirteen patriarchs and thirteen tribes of Israel. There were twelve apostles, often so called, but it is a fact, there were thirteen apostles—Paul was the thirteenth and the greatest. So there were "twelve stars" or States in the woman's crown. And when William Penn surrendered that part of the charter of Delaware in 1703, so that he allowed Pennsylvania and Delaware separate organizations, but still were united under the same proprietary until 1776, then there were also thirteen States that adorned the woman's crown, on the great day of Declaration : corresponding to the thirteen tribes of ancient Israel. See Ezek. xlviii.

3rd. " And upon her head a crown of twelve stars." A "crown" is a symbol of executive authority ; and is so accepted and acknowledged among the nations. It represents the ruling and controlling power in civil government. So that the "crown of twelve stars," or thirteen States, as we have shown, was an ornament to the woman and gave to her beauty and power under executive authority. It was a symbol of her liberty and independence, and not of tyranny and oppression. This " crown " was not a part of the woman ; it was separate and distinct from her ; but was only a part of her adornment with which she was "clothed." So that in, through, and under this " crown " of protection, she could more effectively accomplish her great mission.

We all know that the government of the United States is the outgrowth of the Bible and is a patron, friend, and protector of true religion. Yet while the Church and State are entirely separate, the "crown" represents our civil government, and is a perpetual protection to the Church in her spiritual work of moral elevation and enlightenment of the masses, and in her work of giving liberty to the nations.

4th. "A woman" in symbolic language represents a system of religion or Church. And since this "great wonder" that appeared in heaven, was a woman with "the moon under her feet," we are not left in uncertainty about its meaning. The Church of the Lord Jesus Christ is graphically symbolized. As the life of this symbol was "the woman"; so the life of the government represented by her symbolic crown, is the religion of the Bible, or the Church of the Messiah. The Bible, with its life and liberty, forms the great corner-stone of our body politic. Upon its laws and principles of eternal truth and right stands the grand fabric of our government.

5th. "The woman fled into the wilderness for 1,260 days" or symbolic years. And so it came to pass that the Church was under

persecuting powers for that length of time.
The 1,260 symbolic years reduced to solar
time is exactly 1,451 years and 17 days—filling up the space exactly between the time
that Constantine the Great took the political
headship of the Church, June 17, 325 A. D., ✓
to July 4, 1776, when the *Man-Child* was
born, or "a nation was born in a day." That
was the birthday of the United States. On
that day "the woman" came out of the wilderness, came out from the dens and caves
where she had been hiding for so many centuries from her persecutors and destroyers.
Thank God, the Church will no more be com- ✓
pelled to fly into the wilderness to hide from
her bloody pursuers. The days of the Inquisition and Martyrdom are past. The Man-
Child or this great government, the offspring
of the Church, will forever defend its mother.
Its constitution, its oaths and promises, yea
its very nature compels it to defend the principles of eternal truth and right against all
the combined powers of darkness.

6th. "The great red dragon" of despotism
stood before the woman to devour the Man-
Child as soon as it was born. But the

Almighty providence of God defended it, and saved its life. It is now a young man of an hundred years, full of strength and increasing power; and has already become the dread and glory of the nations and the hope of the world.

7th. "And there was war in heaven," *i. e.*, the place of the Church. "Michael and his angels fought against the dragon; and the dragon fought and his angels." Michael is the type and leader of the angelic hosts battling in God's name against the power of Satan. He was the guardian of the Jewish people in their antagonism to godless power and heathenism. So here, in this prophecy he is represented with his angels as standing up with God's people, the friends of civil and religious liberty, and fighting against the "great red dragon" of despotism and their forces in the dreadful effort to destroy the Man-Child or the establishment of the United States Government. "But they prevailed not; neither was their place found any more in heaven," or in the place of the Church. Despotic power was entirely overthrown in this government, never to be exercised here any more. When our forefathers gained the victory over tyranny in the Revolutionary war, there was unequaled rejoicing all over our country and among oppressed Christians in other lands. I have no doubt it was this grand shout of thanksgiving and praise that John heard, when he heard them saying, "Now is come salvation and strength and the kingdom of our God, and the power of his Christ." This shout would have been nothing in itself, but it was the *beginning* of that victory which God's people are to gain over the despotic powers of earth, and it is to extend from nation to nation, until the kingdoms of this world are declared to be the kingdoms of our Lord and of His Christ. The reason of this great rejoicing and shouting of triumph was because,

8th. "The *accuser* of our brethren is cast down, which accused them before our Lord day and night." Ecclesiastical hierarchy and civil despotism went hand in hand for more than a thousand years. The hierarchy only had to *accuse* God's people to the civil magistrate, of Protestantism, or simply *noncon-formity* to any of their slavish superstitions, when the severest penalties were inflicted. Times without number blood flowed, and martyrs were crowned. Millions and millions perished in this manner. No wonder that heaven and earth shouted together, " when the *accuser* of our brethren was cast down." When " the time of the end " came, such terrible cruelty to God's people could no longer be practiced. These are only some of the coincidences which the careful student may find between the symbol of the Man-Child and the United States.

There is only one serious difficulty in understanding this symbol, and that vanishes before the light of fulfillment, viz: the birth of the Man-child is put *before* the flight of the woman into the wilderness, instead of afterwards. This puzzled commentators all through the interdicted ages. But this is now only a seeming difficulty, and not real. The Lord had sealed up the vision until " the time of the end." And if the chronology of this symbol had been strictly and consecutively followed, then the seal would have been opened, and that would all have been plain hundreds of years ago, which the Lord did not intend to be known and understood aright, until "the time of the end." Now it is as clear as the noonday, so that he that runneth may read. "And there was war in heaven," does not mean in the third heaven, but the place provided for the Church and the friends of human liberty. "Michael and his angels fought against the dragon; and the dragon fought, and his angels, and prevailed not." This is graphic, symbolic language, to represent the terrible conflict that was waged between the Man-Child and his friends, on the one side, and the dragon of despotism and his forces, on the other side ; as was fearfully manifested in the war of the Revolution, which resulted in the establishment of American independence, and the development of the Man-Child of the United States. Take away the gorgeous symbolism of spiritual conflict, and we have the plain history of the war our fathers waged for human liberty and eternal right. This must be the correct interpretation, for there can be no war in the *third* heaven. No dragons, no devils, are there— no, no—all there is joy and peace forever and ever.

Now let us see what *facts* figures can tell
us about this "wonder in heaven" which
John saw. "The woman," or the Church of
God, fled into the wilderness for a time, times
and an half, or for 1,260 days, or years. What
was the occasion of this flight? Was it not
the union of Church and State, or when an
earthly potentate was made head of the
Church, instead of having the Lord Jesus
Christ for head. When did this accursed
politico - ecclesiastical concubinage begin?
Was it not at the Council of Nice, in Bi-
tynia, June 17th A. D. 325, when the Christian religion was made the religion of the
Eastern and Western Empires, under the reign
of Constantine the Great. This at first seemed
a God-send to the Church, but soon the beautiful simplicity of the Church was lost in
pompous rites and ceremonies, and in worldly
honors and emoluments under imperial patronage, and soon the outside kingdom of Christ
was converted into a kingdom of this world.
It was then the woman fled into the wilderness, where she was "nourished" in hidden
and retired places for 1,260 symbolic years.
It was then again in the wilderness that she

had "trial of cruel mockings and scourgings, of bonds and imprisonment." It was then again " they were sawn asunder, were tempted, were slain with the sword, they wandered about in sheep-skins, and goat-skins, being destitute, afflicted, tormented, they wandered in deserts and in mountains and in dens, and caves of the earth," until the *Man-Child* was born. Long had the mother travailed in pain to be delivered, and at last the glorious deliverance came. It was exactly at the time appointed, at the end of " the time, times and an half," or 1,260 symbolic years—"*nechtack*," cut-off, or abbreviated years.

Let us count and see. The 70 weeks of Daniel furnishes us the key. 360 always represents a prophetic year. It may represent a Hebrew year of 364 parts; then 364× 364, is equal to 132,496: then add $\frac{1}{7}$, or Sabbatic time, and we have 151,424. And since 360 is contained in 1,260, three and a half times, then three and a half times one "time," or 151,424, is equal to 529,984 days in solar time, or 1,451 years and 17 days—exactly the time of the sojourn of the woman in the wilderness. Now add 1,451 years and 17 days to June

17th, 325 A. D., and it brings us down exactly
to the setttng up of the Stone Kingdom, or to
the birth of the Man-Child on July 4th, 1776,
when "a nation was born in a day."

These are astonishing facts revealed to us
with the accuracy of the mathematics of
heaven.

CHAPTER IV.

WHERE WILL ISRAEL BE RESTORED?

Or, Where will the "Stone Kingdom" be set up?

ANSWERED BY THE PROPHETS.

THE Scriptures manifestly teach that, in "the latter times," Israel will be restored in a glorious nationality. It has been a favorite notion, both with Jewish and Christian writers, that all these grand prophecies relate to the return of the Jews, and the restoration of Israel in old Palestine. We are not surprised at this notion, because this nationality, to be restored, is called "Israel" by the prophets. This was the best term they had to convey the great idea. They did not say that that nationality was to be made of the friends of civil and religious liberty; not even of Christians. But they said it was to be "Israel."

Gesenius interprets "Israel" to mean "soldier of God." This, then marks the character of that people who should possess the kingdom in the latter days, or the fifth government. They were to be " Israel," or soldiers of God. .

Only disrobe these prophecies of their Jewish paraphernalia, and the proportions and sublimity of Christian republicanism are perfectly delineated. Our blessed Savior has given us a key for their interpretation, Matt. xvii: " His disciples asked him saying, ' Why, then, say the Scribes that Elijah must first come ?' And Jesus answered and said unto them that Elijah is come already, and they knew him not. Then the disciples understood that He spake unto them of *John the Baptist*." Now, when we tell you that the United States is the Stone Kingdom, or Israel restored, suppose you ask the Master by what construction of language do you make out that John the Baptist was Elijah which was for to come, seeing he was altogether another man. John was " the Elijah, which was to come," not because he bore the name, but because he came " in the spirit and power of Elijah." He was therefore declared by the Savior to be indeed the Elijah. If, therefore, a great nationality is promised to arise in the latter days, and the

United States of America exhibits the character, and fills the description, both as to the geography, time, and place of rising, and comes with the spirit and power of Israel, and no other nation under heaven ever has, or ever can answer the description, then we claim that perfect coincidence is perfect fulfillment, and the United States is the nationality promised to Israel in the latter days. The term "Israel" has belonged to the people of God ever since Jacob wrestled with the angel of the Lord. And the Church of God will be called "Israel" till the end of time. Both Jews and Gentiles, when born of the Spirit, become members of God's "Israel." This is triumphantly shown by the Apostle Paul in Rom. iv, and Gal. iii, iv.

It has been suggested that there is one fearful difficulty in the way of this interpretation, *i. e.*, we are too wicked and unworthy a nation to be honored with the title of "Israel." Alas, my brethren, heaven knows our awful wickedness—wickedness in high places and in low places. The Sabbath is desecrated and God's law is despised by millions. But wicked as we are, we are the best people *as a nation* on

the earth. It is the ugly outside of our body-
politic that is daily flared before the world.
Our papers tell of murders, robberies and
high crimes committed all over the continent.
These black parts of history are picked up as
choice morsels to satiate the depraved appe-
tite. The ten thousand acts of kindness, of
benevolence and heroic sacrifice to truth and
duty, are never heard of, and our great throb-
bing heart of humanity, in sympathy with
human woe all round the world, finds no
heralds, no adequate expression, while loud-
mouthed crime tries to drown the praise and
hallelujahs which ascend from the hills and
plains of these "mountains of Israel." Here
the virtuous stranger finds a home and a wel-
come. Here the oppressed of all lands may
find a safe retreat, throw off the yoke of bondage, and enjoy the inheritance of freemen.
Then away with the objection. It is as true
to-day as of old, that "they are not all Israel,
that are of Israel." In "Israel" restored to
nationality, possessed of the true religion and
civil and religious liberty to the full, the
righteous and the wicked, the tares and the
wheat, the wise and the foolish, will be found

together, even unto the judgment day. After
the Lord had led His ancient Israel, a nation of
three millions, from the brick-yards of Egypt
out into the wilderness, with a pillar of cloud
by day and a pillar of fire by night, and they
were gathered around Mt. Sinai to behold the
glory of God, when the lightning rent the mantle
of the sky, and the thunder waxed louder and
louder, when the mountain trembled from its
glowing summit to its granite base—when
from amid such awful grandeur God was giving to Moses the Tables of the Law, where was
Israel? And what was Israel doing? At the
foot of the mountain, making a *golden calf ! !*
and shouting in their idolatrous worship.

Wherefore by the term "Israel restored,"
we mean a providential nation, possessing the
only true religion and a divinely sanctioned
form of government, and possessing territory
sufficient for that great people which is to
have the headship of the world, or leader-
ship in pure religion and civil liberty : a nation,
before whose moral and physical power, monarchy, tyranny, and absolutism are to be
driven away, like chaff before the winds from
the summer threshing floors.

The old notion that "Israel restored," means that the Jews will go back to Palestine, and set up their government in ancient splendor, and turn back the wheels of progress three thousand years, is as false as it is absurd. Many of the Jews will doubtless go back to Palestine, and set up a little republican government. For we think that land was promised to them. But that little, far-off, secluded, part of earth, does not and never can fill the civil, historical, commercial, and geographical description of Israel restored, or the mission of the Stone Kingdom, or the empire of the *Man-Child*, who is to rule the nations with a rod of iron. But the United States of America does fill all the requirements as exactly as the shadow fits the substance. That old notion dishonors the great apostle, when he says "the blindness that has happened to Israel" will continue "until the fullness of the Gentiles is brought in." The Gentiles will be brought in first, and the Jews last—fulfilling what the Master said, "the first shall be last and the last first." In the true Israel, "there is neither Jew nor Greek, there is neither bond nor free, there is neither male nor female, for ye are all *one* in Christ Jesus." "And if ye be Christ's then are ye Abraham's seed, and heirs according to the promise." In view of all this array of testimony as to who Israel is, it is strange, passing strange, that learned American divines, should hold to that old, fitless notion, that "Israel restored" means the return of the Jews to old Palestine : that notion bespeaks more faith than works.

There are a multitude of passages of Scripture, which, as the learned and judicious admit, foretell the rise of a great nationality in the latter times. These predictions cannot, by any just laws of interpretation, be applied to the rise of such nationality in the land of Palestine. But they do most wonderfully apply to and fit the United States of America and no other land under heaven. Let us select a few out of the multitude of descriptions and coincidences that are realized alone in our own great country.

1st. The land of the promised nationality, was to lie *between two seas.* Ezek. xlvii : 18, 20. "From the border unto the east sea. And this is the east side. The west side also shall be the *great sea* from the border. This is the west side." These are exact boundaries of our country. "The west side also shall be the great sea," or Pacific.

If Ezekiel is correct in his geographical description of the land of Israel restored, he certainly cannot refer to Palestine, for there is no sea on its eastern border. And this description must forever prove fatal to that old notion, that the promised nationality is to be in the land of Judea. It lacks an *ocean* on the *east side*.

2nd. Israel was to be *restored*, in a land that had *always been waste.*—Ezek. xxxviii: 8. "The land that is brought back from the sword, and is gathered out of many people, thou shalt come against the mountains of Israel, THAT HAVE BEEN ALWAYS WASTE."— This Scripture is an exact description of our country, and especially that part that speaks of it having been "*always waste.*" A country that had never been cultivated, or improved. This cannot be said of Palestine, for it, in ages past, has been as the garden of the Lord. But our country fully answers the description. When our fathers came to America, they found it a vast wilderness that had been "*always waste.*" The 35th chapter of Isaiah seems to be a grand anthem of praise, and hearty congratulation on their arrival. The earth is represented as shouting for joy, when our forefathers came to take possession of the wilderness. "The wilderness and the solitary place shall be glad for them ; and the desert shall rejoice, and blossom as the rose. It shall blossom abundantly, and rejoice even with joy and singing: the glory of Lebanon shall be given unto it, the excellency of Carmel and Sharon; they shall see the glory of the Lord, and the excellency of our God."

3rd. Our wonderful country is further described, in the same prophecy as having its inhabitants gathered out of the nations, or from many peoples. Not the scattered Jews, gathered from the ends of the earth,—as one nation gathered together. No, no : but it is the description of a land filled with immigrants from all parts of the earth. This is so conspicuous a characteristic of the glorious nationality, that the prophet Isaiah dwells upon it with inspired eloquence. "Lift up thine eyes round about and see ; all they gather themselves together ; they come to thee ; thy sons shall come from far, and thy daughters shall be nursed at thy side." "The abundance of the sea shall be converted (or turned) unto thee ; the forces of the Gentiles shall come unto thee . . . . Who are these that fly as a cloud, and as the doves to their windows? . . . . Thy gates shall be opened continually ; they shall not be shut, day nor night." Truly Isaiah must have seen our country as it now is : with immigrants coming like clouds from all the nations of earth. The whole description is sublimely grand because its fulfillment is the *demonstration* of *truth*. "The sons also of them that afflicted thee, shall come bending unto thee and all they that despise Thee, shall bow themselves down at the soles of Thy feet." The children of those very soldiers that invaded our country, burned our towns, and murdered our people, now come to make our country their home ; and those who sneered at our experiment of popular freedom, and said that our Republic would be buried with Washington, now gladly come and cast in their lot with us, and invest their all under the protection of that banner which they scoffingly said would be the winding-sheet of American independence. How graphic the picture drawn by the pen of inspiration more than 2,500 years ago! As time rolls on, the programme is literally and astonishingly fulfilled.

4th. Extension is one of the characteristics of the promised nationality, Dan. ii : 35, "And the Stone that smote the image became a great mountain and filled the whole earth." Its benign influence, exerted through the transforming power of civil and religious liberty on the nations, will destroy monarchy and absolutism and ultimately fill the whole earth with its heavenly blessings. This will be accomplished, in a great degree, gradually. The leaven of the gospel and human freedom, will work by the power of a divine chemistry, until the whole world shall be leavened. Isaiah, speaking of this government, shortly after its establishment, says, "For thy ruins and thy wastes and thy land of desolation shall even now be too narrow by reason of the inhabitants, and they that swallowed thee up (the autocracies of the old world) shall be far away (beyond the sea). The children

which thou shalt have (in this land) after thou
hast lost the other (ancient Israel) shall say
again in thy ears, 'The place is too strait for
me, give place that I may dwell.'" Extension,
expansion and elevation is the genius of our
institutions. From thirteen States, we now
have thirty-eight States and nine large terri-
tories. Mexico, the West Indies, and all South
America are biding their time to form part of
the great confederacy. Monarchy and mis-
rule melt away in proximity to a glorious republic like icebergs under a tropical sun,
while their natural interests impel them to
seek annexation and to share in the rewards
of a higher development. The magnetism of
human liberty will draw all nations towards
it; while the gospel of Christ adorns it all
with the halo of salvation.

5th. Another famous prophecy to be fulfilled in Israel restored, is in Isaiah xlix : 12,
" Behold these shall come from far, and lo
these from the North and from the West, and
these from the land of Sinim." The learned
generally agree that "Sinim" is China. Sinim, or China, lies due west of our country.
The prophet seems to be astonished at this

wonderful fact, that the Chinese, also, are coming to the land of Israel. China has been a shut-up nation, almost from the days of Noah, and never before, in modern times, mingled with other nations. Now, behold them breaking over their enclosure, and coming from the West. The prophet is amazed at the multitudes coming from every quarter, and especially that the land of "Sinim" should join in the wonderful migration. Hundreds of thousands of them have already come to our hospitable shores, astonishing and startling our people as much as the prophets of old. Now, since these, from the land of Sinim, were to come from the West, how could they have ever reached old Palestine? Palestine never could have been reached by them from that direction, demonstrating that the land of Judea is not to be the place of Israel restored. And since they come from the land of Sinim, and from the West, to our country —in the time appointed —we behold in this a fulfillment of prophecy on a magnificent scale, declaring to the world that the United States of America is the land of Israel restored. Perfect coincidence being perfect fulfillment, our position is demonstrated.

6th. Gog is represented in Ezek. xxxviii: as going up to attack and destroy the glory of Israel restored. Gog says, "I will go up to the land of unwalled villages, I will go to them that are at rest, that dwell safely, all of them dwelling without walls, and having neither bars nor gates, to take a spoil, and to take a prey." Read the whole chapter, and see almost a perfect picture of your own land. I suppose Ezekiel never saw an unwalled city in his life. This description cannot be applied to Judea, for all her cities were walled, from Dan to Beersheba. This famous photograph of prophecy finds a perfect fulfillment in our own prosperous country, where the cities are without walls, gates or bars; where all dwell safely. It finds its perfect fulfillment in the United States, and in no other country on earth, *i. e.*, when we observe all the pointings of prophecy.

7th. *Great intelligence* should mark the progress of the promised nationality, and also a general instruction in divine things. Isaiah liv: 13. "All thy children shall be taught of the Lord; and great shall be the peace of thy children." Is not this an exact foreshadowing of our people ? Our system of free schools is rapidly improving. Academies and Colleges are multiplying all over the land. And our system of Sabbath-school instruction is rapidly becoming a golden net-work in the counties of the States, so that "all thy children shall be taught of the Lord." The minister of the Gospel lifts up his voice in every community. The Bible is unchained and given to the masses, as a light to their feet and a lamp to their path, while the *press* pours forth its countless millions of pages, to teach the people things about the world, as well as about the higher spiritual life. *Great intelligence* among the masses is certainly a characteristic of the people of the United States.

8th. The nationality of Israel restored must be settled in thirteen distinct States, like ancient Israel, only "Joseph should have two portions." Ezek. xlvii : 13. "Thus saith the Lord God. This shall be the border whereby ye shall inherit the land, according to the twelve tribes of Israel :

Joseph shall have two portions."[2] That made thirteen tribes, or States, for ancient Israel. Now it is a remarkable fact that there were twelve States in early colonial times. William Penn held the charter of Pennsylvania and Delaware. And for twenty years the whole territory was governed as the State of Pennsylvania. But in 1703 Delaware obtained a separate organization, while one Governor presided over the Provinces until 1776. Thus the thirteen States were formed. And when we remember that prophecy gives the geographical boundary, and that the eastern border should be on the eastern sea, and the western border should be on the *great western* sea, and when we remember the old colonial charters granted from the Atlantic to the Pacific, we are astounded at the exactness of the prophetic foreshadowing, and the present fulfillment, clearly showing that our country, and no other land on earth can fill the entire programme. It is both sad and *amusing* to see with what *stubbornness* and self-satisfaction many hold to the old ruts of interpretation, *right* or *wrong*. Adam Clarke drew a map of the land of Israel restored, and located it in

Palestine, of course. He made the States all border on the Mediterranean, or western sea, but he could find no eastern sea for the boundary which the prophet called for. Hence the unfitness and absurdity of his position, because it had no "eastern sea" for a boundary.

9th. Our country seems manifestly to be the land lying westward from Judea that the prophet saw, in Chap. 18th, and joyfully saluted. "All hail to the land shadowing with wings, which is beyon1 the rivers of Ethiopia." Where is that land? Let the prophet stand somewhere in Judea, say about Jerusalem, and look beyond the rivers of Ethiopia, beyond the Nile, and its mouths, and we find nothing but a barren desert and the roving Bedouins. Surely that is not what the prophet saw and saluted. Then we must look on in the same direction—for that is specifically given. And we find no other land, or people, on that line of latitude, until we strike the coasts of the Carolinas, in our own country, that could warrant the salutation of the prophet, "All hail to the land." So much for the *direction* in which the prophet tells us to look.

Next, he describes the land as "Shadowing
with wings." The geographical map of North
and South America resembles very much two
great wings—or, perhaps his description referred to the national standard of that people,
which is an eagle, with his wings outspread
from shore to shore. Whatever the prophet
meant, the whole chapter is a wonderful description of our country, and fits it with
astonishing accuracy. Many learned commentators, never dreaming that America had
any place in prophecy, or in God's plans,
acknowledge, as Adam Clarke does, that "this
is the most obscure passage in the whole book
of Isaiah." These learned men look in an
opposite direction from the prophet, and of
course can see nothing. Our interpretation is
certainly legitimate, and the fulfillment should
awaken attention and enkindle our admiration.

10th. There are strong intimations in Scripture that the Stone Kingdom was to be a Republic. Hos. i: 11. The people should be
"gathered together and appoint unto themselves one head," or chief magistrate, appointed by the people. Isaiah i: 26. "And I

will restore thy judges, as at the first, and thy
counsellors as at the beginning." • Ancient
Israel was at first a theocratic republic. And
the government of "Israel restored," from
these passages, would have the right to elect
their own rulers. Also, when the Stone Kingdom was set up, it, at the appointed time,
would break into shivers all forms of monarchy. Also, when ancient Israel asked
Samuel to appoint them a *king*, like the
other nations, the Lord told him to "*protest
solemnly* unto them, and show unto them the
manner of the king that shall reign over
them" and rob them, and degrade them, and
oppress the n. So we see kingly forms of
government exist under the solemn protest of
Almighty God. He alone should be King. He
claims that right among the nations of the
earth. Our conclusion from all this testimony is, that the form of government of the
fifth, and greatest nationality, must be a Republic.

11th. The "waiting isles" of Isaiah is a
sublime announcement of our great country.
"Surely the isles shall wait for me," or the
undiscovered lands shall wait for the develop-

ment of God's providence, "and the ships of Tarshish *first* to bring thy sons from far, their silver and their gold with them unto the name of the Lord thy God, and to the Holy One of Israel, because he hath glorified thee." Tarshish, or Tartessus, formerly a seaport in old Spain. "This opinion," says Mr. Benson, "is now generally adopted by the learned." Here we have the startling announcement that the waiting isles, or undiscovered lands, had been concealed and hid from the avaricious and bloody struggles of the nations, until the set time to favor Zion had come. Then the ships of old Spain would be "*first* to bring thy sons from far." And were not the ships of Spain first to discover, and first to open the way for immigration to, the new world? After Columbus had been repulsed from every court in Europe, did not Ferdinand and Isabella furnish him with the necessary outfit, and thus fulfill their great mission in "first bringing thy sons from far," and so opening to the knowledge of the world our great country? This never can apply to Palestine; for it was not then an undiscovered country. And the ships of

Tarshish or Spain could not be "first" to bring immigration into it. When the minions of monarchy first came to Mexico and Peru and took possession of those countries, they did it in the name of their sovereigns and for the sake of gold. But when the Huguenots, the Quakers, the Puritans and the Covenanters came, it was for conscience's sake, and for the privilege of worshiping God. "Unto the name of the Lord thy God, and to the Holy One of Israel," they came. To write the fulfillment of all this glorious prophecy, would fill a volume. The footsteps of God's providence in all our history from its discovery to the time when "a nation was born at once," July 4, 1776, and on through all our struggles to the present, are as visible as was the pillar of cloud by day and the pillar of fire by night which led old Israel into the promised land.

12th. The infancy of restored Israel should receive "royal patronage," Isa. xlix: 23. "And kings shall be thy nursing fathers, and their queens thy nursing mothers." Nursing applies to infancy, and all through our early history the various sovereigns of Europe gave a fostering hand to colonization.

In our helpless infancy, their kings were our
nursing fathers, and their queens were our
nursing mothers. And in honor of them,
several of the old thirteen States were named,
and numberless counties and towns and places
—Virginia, Georgia, Maryland and the Caro
linas among the States, and of counties, King
William, Prince George, Prince Edward and
a multitude of royal names, that will forever
perpetuate the fulfillment of prophecy that
royalty should be our foster-parent.

13th. *Coming events cast their shadows before them.* The Continental Congress, in 1782,
adopted a device for the great seal of the
United States, and re-adopted it in 1789. The
obverse side is familiar to all, but the reverse
side which was adopted, we have no evidence
that it was ever made or used. But in its
adoption we see the hand of Providence fixing
in the ægis of our country its glorious prophecy—telling great truths which its framers,
Daniel-like, wrote but did not comprehend.
In the centre there is an unfinished pyramid
of thirteen layers of large hewn *stones*, on the
base of which is inscribed "1776." High
above this pyramid is a triangular apex, in

the centre of which is represented the all-see-
ing Eye, overlooking all.   Above it is this inscription—"Annuit Coeptis," and underneath
the circle—"Novus ordo seclorum."   All of
which may be translated, "Providence favors
the beginning of the new order of the ages."
Could a more beautiful, appropriate or befitting device have been made for the Great Seal
of State for the Stone Kingdom, which was
then set up?   We see in it the symbolic Stone
cut out of the mountain.   We see in it the
symbol of God's wonderful providence.   And
we have in it the sublime announcement of
the beginning of "the new order of the ages,"
when men would be free, when the Bible would
be unchained, and when religion would be un-
trammeled by popes and priests and civil despots.   Truly

> "God moves in a mysterious way
> His wonders to perform."

And now, my countrymen, with such a history as ours, guided in every step of our progress by the hand of Providence ; in the pangs
of the birth of the Man-Child, a safe deliverance
granted; when the dragon of despotism endeavored to destroy us, His providence saved

us; then such men as He gave us, in Cabinet
and Camp, for those times of trial, in the form-
ative period of our government, "Their like
we ne'er shall see again"—then an hundred
years of unequalled prosperity, marred only
by a few years of civil war! Your country
now moves forward with a giant's tread to the
first place amongst the nations of the earth.
Her divine programme is written, and her destiny is glorious. See to it, my countrymen,
that you act well your part. Do honor to
yourselves—to your country—and to your
God. "Then Gentiles and kings shall see thy
glory, and thou shalt be called by a *new name.*
Thy sun" (or civil government) "shall no
more go down; neither shall thy moon" (the
blessings of the Church) "withdraw itself; for
the Lord shall be thine everlasting Light, and
the days of thy mourning shall be ended."
"A little one shall become a thousand, and a
small one a strong nation; I the Lord will
hasten it in His time."

CHAPTER V.

THE TWO AMERICAS,

Or " The Land Shadowed with Wings."—*Isaiah xviii.*

THIS chapter has been a puzzle to commentators through all the ages. Dr. Scott says, "This is one of the most obscure prophecies in the Scriptures." Adam Clarke says, " It is the most difficult chapter in the whole book." Addison Alexander says, "Nearly every word and phrase of this difficult verse, (he might well have said, chapter) has been the subject of discordant explanations."

There are two reasons why this prophecy could not be understood at an earlier time. 1st. The Lord had *sealed it up* till " the time of the end." Dan. xii. 9. All through the interdicted ages the seal could not be broken, and this prophecy could not be understood. No wonder that King James' translators could make no sense out of this chapter. The seal *then* had not been broken. 2nd. The learned theologians and commentators of Europe never could see any of God's plans or prophecies reaching to America. This third part of the earth's surface is left outside of His dominions —especially outside of His prophecy and the programme of the nations. And still the sharp-cut and distinctly-drawn prophecies of this chapter could find no counterpart anywhere in the Old World. Hence European commentators, and those who follow in their tracks, are puzzled. After Herculean labors to interpret it satisfactorily, they gave it up in despair. God's prophet looked across the Atlantic and saw glorious things. But these learned theologians looked in another quarter, and of course could see nothing that the prophet saw, and described so graphically.

But by looking on in the same line with the prophet we find an interpretation that fits the prophecy as substance fits the shadow. Perfect coincidence is perfect fulfillment. Let us examine and see what saith the Lord, and what say His works and providence.

V. 1. "Ho! to the land shadowing with

wings, which is beyond the rivers of Ethiopia." "Ho," in this connection, is an interjection of exhortation or salutation, equivalent to the Latin *Salve!* Hail! and not a "woe," as in the English Version. The prophet was somewhere in Palestine, probably in Jerusalem, as he looked out west across the rivers of Ethiopia—the Nile or its mouths (anciently the river had seven mouths, ninety or a hundred miles in length)—and saw the land described. Surely this land is not in Africa, for beyond the Nile he could see nothing but the sandy desert and the roving Bedouins. But the course is specific: therefore we must look on in the same direction, on the same parallel of latitude, across the Atlantic, and the first land we find is North America, about the coast of the Carolinas. This land corresponds exactly with the prophet's description. Take a large map of North and South America, and you will find that those two great divisions wonderfully resemble two huge wings. And it seems evident that this is the land shadowed with wings which the prophet saw, and no other. Also the ensign or flag of the United States has an eagle with its wings outstretch-

ed from shore to shore. Truly America is the
land shadowed with wings which Isaiah saw.
It lies in the direction pointed out, and corresponds exactly with the description given.

V. 2. "That sendeth on the sea vessels of
revolvings, and that drink up upon the face of
the waters." The word translated "ambassa-
dors" in the common version in Hebrew is
tserem, and means to go in a circle—to re-
volve—and the noun derived from it means "a
hinge," with the idea of revolving. Then in
the plural it means "writhings"—throes—or
groanings—as of a woman in travail. Now
this word describes something that goes on
the sea. The next descriptive word is *gomea*, translated "bulrushes." But this Hebrew word is singular and means "a bulrush."
It is therefore manifest that this translation is
not the proper one, for surely the prophet did
not mean to say "vessels of a bulrush." But
the word *gomea* is derived from *ga-ma*, which
means "to absorb"—"to drink up"—"to
swallow." Now put the two words together,
and see what sort of vessels are to sail on the
seas to this land of prophecy. "That sendeth
on the sea vessels of revolvings, and that

drink up." Anyone who has traveled on a steamship or on a steamboat knows how the escaping steam groans as if in pain, while the great wheels or screw-propeller revolves. "And vessels that drink up." The engine must be constantly drinking water to supply the steam. Do not these two words, "tse-rem" and "gomea," so pregnant with meaning, give an astonishingly accurate description of steam vessels, as they now go on the face of the waters?

"Go ye swift messengers to a nation tall and naked, to a people terrible from their begining, and far away, to a nation most mighty, treading down their enemies." This is a remarkably life-like picture of the aborigines of our country. "To a nation tall and naked." The Indians are notable for their erectness of stature. They also have little or no beard—smooth-faced. "Naked" may also refer to their having little or no clothing. "To a people terrible since they existed" fierce and war-like "and far away." *Va-ha-le-ah.* This word is strangely left out of King James' translation altogether. It is connected in the clause by the copulative conjunction *rav* to give emphasis to further description; and it most significantly points to the land and the people that were " far away " beyond the sea. " To a people most mighty, and treading down their enemies "—uncompromising and relentless. Three hundred and fifty years ago, there were countless thousands of this people in America. The Aztec dynasty was immense under the reign of the Montezumas. Also, there were many other powerful tribes in North America, and the empire of the Incas in Peru, and other mighty nations in South America. So that the description of the prophet is not only graphic, but astonishingly accurate, as the fulfillment has shown. The history of the aboriginal nations of America is a thrilling commentary on this portion of prophecy.

" Whose land the streams (or floods) divide." What land? The land " shadowed with wings." The land occupied by " a people tall and naked, and terrible from their beginning and far away." It is North and South America that the "*streams divide.*" Please remember that if you draw a straight line, North and South, along the western coast

of Florida, South America lies entirely east
of that line, and the Gulf of Mexico west.
What "streams" or floods divide these lands?
The great oceanic current of the North Atlantic, called the Gulf Stream, flows in a north-
easterly direction, along the coast of North
America, south of Greenland and Iceland,
and then east to the western coast of Europe,
then deflecting south by Spain, and then by
the north-western coast of Africa and the
Canary islands, then south-west across the
Atlantic, by the mouth of the Amazon, then
north-west along the coast of South America,
where it strikes the West India Islands, and
divides into two great parts, or halves. The
south part flows through the Carribbean sea,
and sweeps round the entire coast of the Gulf
of Mexico, and out at the Straits of Florida,
fifty miles wide, 3,000 feet deep and at a ve-
locity of four miles per hour, and thence up in a
north-easterly course, where it joins the other
half, that flows north of the West Indies. And
thus on and on, in an everlasting stream, and
round and round, forming a vast circuit, part
of which forever divides "the land shadowed
with wings." You perceive one half of this

" stream " is *doubled* like a great *loop*, as it
flows into the Gulf of Mexico at one place
and out at another. Hence—*na-ha-rem*—
streams, is plural, so that in going from North
America to South America you *must* cross
the " stream " twice. Hence the prophet
said " whose land the STREAMS (or floods)
divide." Who can doubt the inspiration of
God's Word, when he reads this description,
given 2,500 years ago, of " the undiscovered
lands "? To-day we find the land and the
"*streams*" *exactly* as the prophet described
them.

V. 3. " All ye inhabitants of the world and
dwellers on the earth, when he lifteth up a
banner on these mountains, ye shall see, and
ye shall hear when he bloweth the trumpet."

This verse invites the attention of the world
to some great event. In the preceding verses
the land and its inhabitants were minutely
described. Now the great event referred to,
is to take place when a banner is " lifted up
upon these mountains " of Israel restored, and
when the trumpet is sounded. By this we
understand that a great civil and military
movement will be inaugurated, that will so

change the face of the country, and, through a long series of years, will constantly sweep away the aboriginal inhabitants, until "the inhabitants of the world, and dwellers on the earth shall see" and behold with astonishment the wonderful results. In the days of Cortez and Pizarro, the banner was first "lifted up," and from that day to the present time, the trumpet of war has often sounded long and loud among the mountains and plains of North and South America: until the countless millions that once claimed this land as theirs, are now gathered with the pale nations of the dead. Only a few thousands are left, to tell how fearful and fatal the war has been, for more than 350 years. As when Joshua led ancient Israel into old Canaan, the land of promise, and swept away the inhabitants, took possession of their towns and country, and established the thirteen tribes in the conquered territory, and became a great nation for more than a thousand years—so when "the time of the end" had come, when the Pilgrims, and Huguenots, and Quakers, and Covenanters, and all the persecuted for conscience's sake were flying to these shores, "the banner was lifted up" on these mountains of Israel restored, and the trumpet was sounded for relentless war. Then the Lord gave us Washington, to lead our forces through trials and blood on to victory. The thirteen States of Israel were restored and established. Thus the great Republican Confederacy began, and for a hundred years has been growing in power and influence, until "all the nations of the earth" are now beholding with astonishment the wonderful results. This seems to be the true meaning of this hitherto difficult passage, now so clear, so plain.

4th. "For thus saith Jehovah to me ; I will rest, [or remain quiet] and will look [as a mere spectator] on my dwelling-place, as the bright heat of the sun, as a cloud of dew in the heat of harvest." As the bright heat of the sun and dewy clouds ripen the various crops which require time to bring about maturity, so the Lord said "I will rest and look upon my dwelling-place" for more than 2.000 years: that, during all those ages, my purposes may be accomplished, and my plans brought to full maturity. Hence America was undiscovered for so many centuries, until the set

time to favor Zion had come. When monarchy had done its best, or worst, and utterly
failed to elevate, enlighten, and bless the
masses of mankind, then America was discovered, and the "Stone Kingdom" was set
up, to be a blessing to the suffering millions
of earth. All through the long ages of the
world—ages of experiment in monarchy—
ages of failure to bring forth the ripe fruit of
civil and religious liberty—ages of despotism
—ages of martyrdom and blood—ages that
were necessary, it is true, to teach the world
the glory of the Christian religion and human
freedom—all through these ages, God's eternal
plans were being fulfilled, preparatory to the
setting up of the government of *Israel Restored*, in the *Fifth Nationality.*

V. 5. "For before the harvest, when the
bloom is full, and before the blossom becomes
ripened grapes, he cuts off the twigs with pruning knives, and the tendrils he casts out that
he cuts off." With this treatment of a vineyard, no fruit could ripen. Notwithstanding
the bloom is abundant, and the outlook most
hopeful, yet if pruning knives cut off all the
twigs bearing grapes, the vineyard is, and

must be, fruitless. So with this land, during all the long ages that it was "waiting," undiscovered. Notwithstanding its vast resources and blooming prospects, it brought forth no fruit to maturity—no ripened offerings to the praise of Almighty grace.

V. 6. "They shall be left together to the wild birds of the mountains and to the wild beasts of the land, and wild birds shall summer thereon, and all the wild beasts of the land shall winter thereon." This is expressive of utter neglect, and desolation. This place of the Church, in "the land shadowed with wings," was left for ages to the wild birds of the mountains and to the wild beasts of the land, waiting the march of Providence and the fulfillment of prophecy.

V. 7. "At that time a gift shall be offered to Jehovah of Hosts—a people tall and naked, and from a people terrible from their beginning, and far away—a nation most mighty, and treading down their enemies, whose land *streams* [or floods] divide, to the place of the name of Jehovah of Hosts—Mount Zion."

"At that time"—when His banner is lifted up upon these mountains, after countless wait-

ing ages—when the Stone Kingdom is set up,
a gift shall be brought to Jehovah of Hosts of
" a people tall and naked." Thus one nation
is represented as bringing another nation in
its arms and offering it to Jehovah of Hosts.
And have not the Churches of the United
States sent out the Gospel to the Indian
tribes, from the earliest times, and whole
tribes have been civilized and Christianized?
Thus fulfilling the prophecy of one nation
offering another as a *gift* to Jehovah of
Hosts. And then they in their turn are
represented as bringing gifts to the Lord of
Hosts. In this ancient Israel differs from
Israel restored. Whereas, the one was ordered
to drive out *all* the Canaanites, and make no
alliance with them, the other offers some of
the tribes as a gift to the Lord of Hosts—" to
the place of the name of Jehovah of Hosts—
Mount Zion," *i. e.*, to the place of His Church,
and where His glory is manifested.

CHAPTER VI.

BOUNDARIES OF THE LAND OF ISRAEL RE-STORED GIVEN.

Its Division into Thirteen States.—*Ezek. xlvii. xlviii.*

"THUS saith the Lord Jehovah. This shall be the border whereby ye shall inherit the land *according* to the twelve tribes of Israel. Joseph shall have two portions—(*i. e.*, in all thirteen States.) And ye shall inherit it one as well as another; concerning the which I lifted up my hand, to give it unto your fathers; and this land *shall fall unto* you for inheritance. And this shall be the border of the land toward the north side from the great sea." . . . Then follows a number of names on this north border, that correspond in part with the Mosaic division in Numbers. These names in Ezekiel's division must be symbolic, for this line extends to the east sea: but in the Mosaic division there was no east sea for an eastern border. "And

88

the east side ye shall measure . . . .
from the border unto the east sea. And this
is the east side. And the south side, southward from the palm-tree, *tamar*, even to the
waters of strife, (south of) the consecrated
possession to the great sea. And this is the
south side, southward." Notice how definitely this south boundary is given. " The west
side also shall be the great sea. . . . .
This is the west side. So shall you divide
this land unto you, according to the tribes of
Israel. And it shall come to pass that ye
shall divide it by lot, for an inheritance unto
you, and to the strangers that sojourn among
you, which shall beget children among you:
and they shall be unto you as born in the
country, among the children of Israel; they
shall have inheritance with you among the
tribes of Israel. And it shall come to pass
that, in what tribe the stranger sojourneth,
there shall ye give him his inheritance, saith
the Lord God."

Then, in the 48th chapter, we find the names
of all the thirteen tribes, with their portion of
land assigned to each, running from east to west.
The portion of Levi lay between Judah and

Benjamin. The inspired writer, in drawing a map of the country, mentions the course of each portion, stating that it must run from east to west. This fact is expressed with great emphasis. So that all the portions extended from the sea on the east, to the great sea on the west. Dr. Scott says "As no such division took place after the captivity, this must be understood of future events. This division of the land differs entirely from that which was made in the days of Joshua; and it is not probable that it should ever literally take place." Of course this division of the land can never take place in old Palestine, because it will always lack borders. It will always lack an eastern sea for a boundary, and also a sea on the south side. But there is a country that Ezekiel and Isaiah and Daniel and John saw, that fills the bill *exactly;* that furnishes an "eastern sea, and the great western sea." And "the south side, southward from the palm-tree [or place of palm-trees] unto the waters of strife [or the stormy Gulf of Mexico south of] the consecrated possession unto the great sea. And this is the south side, southward." The south boundary of the United States is astonishingly accurately given. And on the north, "the border from the sea shall be surrounded with clouds, *hazar-enon*, the border of the traffic, *damasek*, and north northward, and the border a fortress, *hamath*, and this is the north side." The Hebrew names used in the boundaries of Israel restored, must be symbolic. It would not have done to have given the literal names of the present borders, for then the prophecy would have been understood before the seal was broken, and before the period of " the time of the end " had come. But now " the time of the end " has come, and we may legitimately inquire for the symbolic meaning.

Next let us point out some of the coincidences between Israel restored, as described by Ezekiel in chapters xlvii: and xlviii: and the United States, and see how the description fits our land.

1st. The north boundary of the United States, beginning on the Pacific coast: this is specifically mentioned " from the great sea " on the west, and coming east the border is "surrounded with clouds " for more than a

1,000 miles through the Rocky Mountains. This may mean political clouds, as the fulfillment shows, as well as clouds of vapor. Then by "the border of traffic." This may mean the limit of trade and commerce on the North, as it is in some parts of the line; or it may mean "the border of traffic" on the great Lakes between British America and the United States—then on through "pine forests" to "the east sea," or Atlantic: this fully corresponds with "the pine forests" of Maine, and all that region. But there are other Hebrew words named in this border, to the roots of which lexicographers fail to give us any clue, or any satisfactory signification: which reminds us that the north border is "surrounded with clouds," which may not be cleared away till after the coming storm, spoken of by the prophets. And as the north boundary, in Ezekiel's field notes, is "surrounded with clouds" and much uncertainty, so was the north boundary of the United States for a long time a subject of great perplexity. In these and other points, the shadow and the substance coincide.

2nd. The south side of the United States,

beginning at Florida, or place of " the palm
tree." *Tamar*, is a generic term, and has many
species, some of which grow in Florida, and
probably all might be cultivated successfully.
From thence along the coast of " the waters
of strife," or the stormy Gulf, which bounds
on the south, " the consecrated possession,"
and then on to " the great sea," or Pacific
ocean, I presume on the same latitude, since
all the tribes had their portion marked out.
side by side of each other, from the east to
the west. The southern boundary must also
be correspondingly straight from east to west.
This is a remarkable coincidence. On the
south side, the Gulf of Mexico is graphically
described as " the waters of strife," or stormy,
lying south of " the consecrated possession,"
or land of Israel restored.

3rd. " The east side ye shall measure from
the border . . . unto the east sea. And
this is the east side." In like manner, the
Atlantic ocean lies on the east side of our
country, and corresponds to " the east sea," as
seen in Ezekiel's vision and map of survey.

4th. " The west side shall also be the
great sea." This corresponds *exactly* with

the Pacific ocean on the west border of America. The shadow and the substance fit with wonderful exactness. " The great sea " and the Pacific ocean coincide.

5th. The land in all the thirteen tribes, as written in the prophecy, must be laid out from east to west. And as shown from the field-notes of the boundaries, the portion of land for each tribe must be measured from "the east sea " to " the great sea " on the west—from the Atlantic to the Pacific. This plan of division, for each portion, is specifically given. Now let us behold with wonder the coincidence between this vision and our own thirteen States, in their beginning. In 1663, Charles II., King of England, granted the province of Carolina to eight noblemen. It lay between 29° and 36° 30′ north latitude. This embraced all of North Carolina, South Carolina and Georgia, three of the old thirteen States. And the territory of this grant extended east and west, "from the Atlantic to the Pacific," coinciding with the divine pattern, although the contracting parties cared nothing and knew nothing about the divine programme.

In 1609, James I., King of England, granted the province of Virginia to the London Company. The grant was to reach 200 miles north of Old Point Comfort, and 200 miles south, and to extend from the Atlantic to the Pacific. This embraced Virginia and Maryland, two more of the old thirteen States, and brings them in for a full share of the territory.

About 1615, King James I. granted a patent to Captain John Smith for a colony, called "New England." It was all that territory lying between 46' and 48' north latitude Joining the grant to the "London Company" on the south, it extended from the Atlantic to the Pacific, covering all the territory of the other eight States of the old thirteen—and extended "from the east to the west." There were other charters granted which lapped and interlapped. But enough has been written to show that the grants to the original thirteen States, extended from "the east sea" to "the great sea" on the west, coinciding perfectly with the division of the land that Ezekiel saw and surveyed. However strange these coincidences may appear, they are no less strange than true. "Man's heart deviseth his way, but the Lord directeth his steps."

6th. Another remarkable coincidence is, the portions of all the thirteen tribes of Israel began their settlements on the east side, and moved on to the west, according to the vision of Ezekiel. And just so in Israel restored, they all began on the east side, on the Atlantic coast, and moved on with settlement and civilization to the west, or Pacific. Surely this is not the work of chance, but the execution of a grand plan, directed by the hand of Providence. Here we see multitudes of men of different nationalities, unwittingly carrying out the divine programme, revealed more than 2,500 years ago. Truly the Bible is God's word, written by omniscience.

7th. Another coincidence is, there were twelve tribes in Israel, but Joseph had two tribes, making thirteen. So in the United States there were twelve States. But Pennsylvania and Delaware, William Penn's two States, were under one governor, or proprietary, although they each had a separate and distinct Assembly, from 1703 to 1776, Then they became separate and independent States, which make up the thirteen. This wonderful coincidence was not of chance, but the workings of an eternal plan. "So shall ye divide the land unto you, *according* to the tribes of Israel." And so it has been. The divine pattern has been followed and realized in the great Restoration.

8th. "In what tribe the stranger sojourneth, there shall ye give him his inheritance, saith the Lord God." This pointed to an enlarged condition from one family, to all the families of earth under the Christian dispensation. When men become *Christians*, then they become *Israelites*, and *children* of *Abraham*, and are entitled to their inheritance. In whatever tribe [or State] the stranger sojourneth, there he may have his inheritance. And so it is in the United States; strangers may come from all parts of the world, and cast in their lot with us, and purchase for themselves an inheritance, and be protected by the laws of the country. "And ye shall inherit it one as well as another": there can be no difference between the Jew and the Gentile in Christian Israel. This prophecy clearly describes the restoration "in the latter days," under the expanding glory of the Gospel dispensation.

when the children of Shem, Ham and Japheth, shall become by faith the seed of Abraham, true Israelites, and heirs according to the promise. Thus the Land and the Church are strangely connected—the civil and the religious seem to go hand in hand all through the enlarged condition of the great restoration. So in this prophecy there is a particular land assigned to Israel, with metes and bounds given it, and the number of States specified, to *begin with*. And this last vision of Ezekiel corresponds with the Stone which was cut out of the mountain without hands. It was to increase and increase, until it became a great mountain, and filled the whole earth. This last vision also corresponds with " *the ancient of days*," who came after the four beasts which Daniel saw. When he came he had but 3,000,000 to minister unto him, but he had " a rod of *iron* given to him, to rule all nations," and to fill the earth with his glory. In like manner, this wonderful vision of Ezekiel closes with a small beginning of thirteen States, to start the world on a higher plane of development. But small as its beginnings were, its mission is to reach to,

and bless the ends of the earth with liberty
and life.

The power of the Gospel through this
people is demonstrated in the same chapter,
by the water which Ezekiel saw flowing from
the house and the altar, small at first; but
further down, the stream became deeper, even
to the ankles; and further on, it came to the
knees; still flowing with an increasing swell,
" the waters were to the loins"; still flowing
with a widening sweep and a rising power, it
became " a river that could not be passed
over." So with the unnoticed and despised
waters of life and liberty, which flowed first
from the land of Israel's restoration. This
stream of influence is widening and deepening
in its flow. There is a divine power about it
that elevates the human mind, and gives it
higher aspirations. And the trees that grow
on either bank of this river, bear fruit for the
nourishment of the people: and their leaves
are " for the healing of the nations." This
stream has power to bear down and sweep
away all tyranny, oppression, and every
thing that opposes civil and religious liberty.
When this government was not half a century

old, the stream of its influence shook terribly, either directly or indirectly, every throne in Europe. If such was the effect of this stream, when so small, what will the surging floods do? Surely the beginning is hopeful, but the ending will be the glory of the world. The prophet tells us "the greatness of the kingdom under the whole heaven, shall be given to the people of the saints of the Most High, whose kingdom is an everlasting kingdom, and all dominions shall serve and obey Him."

CHAPTER VII.

THE CHURCH

And the Land of Her Restoration.—*Isa. xlix. 11-26.*

IN this chapter we have some most cheering prophecies of the Church, of her deliverance from oppression, of her wonderful enlargement and glorious triumphs; also, of the land of Israel, or the place of the Church's ✓ restoration—our own United States—of her great development of physical resources and political power: all these are graphically foreshadowed by the prophet, and their reality is demonstrated by fulfillment.

V. 11. "I will appoint all my mountains for a highway, and my roads shall be made high." The language here implies that gathering armies would soon be on the march to this land described. The preparations were vast, but not greater than necessary. As "the mountains of Israel" is an expression frequently used for the whole land of ancient Israel, so in this prophecy we take "all my mountains" to mean all my mountains of Israel restored, or the whole land. The word *umsillotha* means a way cast up—a causeway—built with timbers across the road. May this not mean the system of railroads which the prophet saw in these times, then "far off," that is now forming a network all over our country from sea to sea? Are not these pre-eminently highways, over which all the armies of immigrants pass which come to us from every quarter of the globe?

"My roads shall be made high." There will be ample room for Christians of every name to come without fear of persecution. They need no longer hide in dens and caves and in secret places in the wilderness for fear. But here they may travel openly on the great highways, fearing no more the blood-hounds of cruelty which so often yelped on their track. Here they may worship God as they please.

The Church and the land of the Church seem intimately connected in all these prophecies. Not that all the people in this land are or will be Christians, any more than that all the Jews in ancient Israel were Israelites. For in Israel restored, as well as in ancient Israel, millions of devils in human shape may be found. Ancient Israel, in the days of Ahab and Jezebel, was almost entirely swallowed up in idolatry. Elijah described those times plaintively : " For the children of Israel have forsaken Thy. covenant, thrown down Thine altars and slain Thy prophets with the sword ; and I, even I, only am left, and they seek my life to take it away." This is indeed a sad picture. The objection that this country is too wicked to be Israel restored falls to the ground when compared and contrasted with ancient Israel under such rulers as Ahab and Jezebel and Manasseh and Jeroboam and others of like character.

V. 12. " Behold these shall come from far off, and behold these from the north and from the west, and these from the land of Sinim."

The prophet had just declared that " all my mountains " shall be appointed for " a highway." And now he calls the attention of the world to " behold these shall come from far off, and behold these from the north [of Europe] and from the west [of Europe]." The fulfillment shows this, and the facts in the case are better interpreters of the Scripture than vague, *a priori* theories. Behold great multitudes coming from every quarter of the compass to the land of restoration. Multitudes fleeing from tyranny and oppression and coming to a land of civil and religious liberty, to a land of an open Bible and great physical prosperity and of inexhaustible resources, to a land where the Lord alone is King of the conscience. What land on earth can this be but our own United States? To no other land on earth is so great a migration directing the march of its moving millions—to the Stone Kingdom, to the great fifth nationality, or to Israel restored, just as the prophets foretold.

"And these from the land of Sinim." Commentators are generally agreed that Sinim, or Sina, is China. The prophet beholds with astonishment vast multitudes coming from every quarter but especially "these from the land of Sinim," or China. That great country has been exclusive and shut up to itself for thousands of years, not mingling and commingling with other nations in religion or commerce, but behold, even its people are breaking over

their barriers and by some strange impulse
are joining the great migration. Hundreds of
thousands have already come to our shores
from the west. Their coming has startled our
people even more than was the prophet. These
are times of wonderful fulfillment of wonderful
prophecies. " These from the land of Sinim,"
coming "from the west" shows that old Palestine never could be the land of restoration
spoken of, because the Chinese never could
reach that land from that direction ; but coming from the west, across the Pacific, of course
they must land on our western coast, as they
have done by scores of thousands. All this
prophecy points to the United States as restored Israel with unerring accuracy. Its fulfillment is its own demonstration.

V. 13. "Shout, O heavens, and rejoice, O
earth, let the mountains break forth into joy!
because Jehovah has comforted His people,
and He will have compassion on His afflicted."
The prophet saw the panorama of God's providence passing. It seemed to him as already
realized. He saw the Church coming out of
the wilderness, from her long afflictions and
horrible persecutions. He saw God's Church,

or Israel, restored to more than ancient glory
in their own land, together with millions of
the oppressed of earth who had longed and
prayed for civil and religious liberty to develop their resources according to their convictions of right.   He saw them coming from
every quarter to build up their own great
nationality—the fifth and last form of government which was to be developed with increas·
ing glory from age to age.   They were flushed
with hope and joyful expectation.   The pros-
pect was transcendently glorious in the history of earth.   Hence he calls upon the heavens to shout and the earth to rejoice and the
mountains to break forth into joy, " because
Jehovah had comforted His people and had
compassion on His afflicted."

V. 14. " And yet Zion said, Jehovah hath
forsaken me, and the Lord hath forgotten me."
How natural for us to complain in the midst
of affliction.   Zion, or the Church of God, had
been sorely tried and terribly afflicted for
many long centuries. She had been tyrannized
over, robbed and oppressed so long ; her beautiful garments had been so often torn or burned
with fire or bespattered with her own blood ;

and all her brightest earthly hopes seemed so utterly blasted, that she said, "All these things are against me"—"Jehovah hath forsaken me, and the Lord hath forgotten me." The glorious change described above was not the result of the Church's confidence in her God, for she said, "The Lord hath forgotten me," but it is a grand illustration of the divine sovereignty in carrying out His eternal programme for His own glory and for the infinite betterment of His people, both as to civil government, to bless the world thereby with larger liberty, and also in an infinitely greater manner to promote the glory of His redemption.

V. 15. "Will a woman forget her sucking child, from having compassion on the son of her womb? Also even these will forget, and yet I will not forget thee." The unfailing and constant affection of God for His children is here eloquently expressed. A mother may forget her child, but "I will not forget thee." The tenderest ties known on earth may be broken, but "I will not forsake thee."

V. 16. "Behold, upon both palms I have engraven thee; thy walls are always before me." 'It is impossible for me to forget thee or the promises I have made to thee. Both my blood-bought Church and the land of her restoration are ever before me. My promises, though extended through thousands of years, are not forgotten. Their fulfillment, though long delayed, shall gloriously and literally come to pass.'

V. 17. "Thy sons hasten to thee. Thy wasters and thy destroyers shall go out from thee," *i. e.*, depart from thee. "Thy sons hasten to thee" is another announcement of the great migration that has set in to the land of the promised restoration. Has not this prophecy been, and is it not now being, wonderfully realized? Many thousands are hastening to our shores from all parts of the world. "Thy sons" does not imply that all the host of immigrants are Christians, or ever will be, any more than that all the "sons of Israel" were pious. For the country must be developed and the government must be made powerful. Both Church and State, though separate and distinct, must flourish in this land to accomplish their great mission ecclesiastically, politically and revolutionary among the nations.

An absolutely holy nation will never be found on this earth, not even in the noontide of the millennial reign. Such an ideal nation is without precedent or prophecy and is sublimated utopianism.

"Thy wasters and thy destroyers shall go out from thee." The British armies that wasted our people for so many years and opposed the establishment of our government and our matchless system of civil and religious liberty, have gone out from us. They fought against the providence of God, and that providence was too strong for them. The fierce and warlike Indian tribes that wasted our forefathers and destroyed their property, have gone out from us. They have wasted away, until now scarcely a shadow of their former greatness is left to witness the astonishing fulfillment of this part of the eternal programme.

V. 18. "Lift up thine eyes round about and see, all of them are gathered together, they are come to thee. As I live, saith Jehovah, that all of them as an ornament thou shalt put on and bind them as a bride." This seems to be a glimpse of the promised country further on in its history than was seen in the preceding verses. It represents the land as already occupied by many thousands, with all the equipments of the Church and a well-regulated government. "As I live, saith Jehovah, that all of them as an ornament thou shalt put on, and bind them as a bride." Thus by this great multitude of forces all parts of the land of the Church shall be made beautiful, by improved agriculture, by a thrifty population, by schools and churches, by sobriety and virtue, while the land and the people enjoy their Sabbaths—all, even all these, "shall be put on and bound to her, as doeth a bride her beautiful ornaments." Then the Church with her propitious surroundings shall "look forth as the morning, fair as the moon, clear as the sun, and terrible as an army with banners."

V. 19. "Then thy ruins and thy wastes and thy desolated land, even at this time, thou shalt be too narrow for the inhabitants, and they that swallowed thee up shall be far away." This difficult passage seems to mean; instead of a land that was once for untold centuries, waste and ruins and desolation, now, because of the great influx of inhabitants, is too narrow. Its prosperity is so great, more territory is demanded. It is no longer wastes and ruins and desolation, but crowded with millions and enlivened with the bustle of labor and commerce : more room and more territory are needed for its increasing and prosperous multitudes. "They that swallowed thee up"—the autocracies and armies of the old world, " shall be far away " —beyond the seas, so that they cannot hinder thy growth or impede thy progress.

V. 20. " Again the children which thou shalt have after thou hast lost the other [ancient Israel] shall say in thine ears, the dwelling-place is too narrow for me, give place to me that I may dwell." Enlargement, exten-sion and expansion, is a prominent characteristic of Israel restored. "The Stone that smote the image, became a great mountain, and filled the whole earth." The adjoining countries and nations will see the light of Israel's growth and partake of its nature and character. And thus the leaven will work, extending her borders further and wider, while the aggressive cry of conquest will be heard in every direction, " Give place. Make

room for me, that I may dwell." The dwelling place of the Church is to be co-extensive
with her conquests ; and ultimately to em
brace the whole world. Such is the divine
programme. All "the thrones are to be cast
down," and "the saints of the Most High
shall take the kingdom and possess the kingdom forever, even forever and ever."

V. 21. "And thou shalt say in thy heart,
Who hath begotten for me even these, seeing
I have lost my children, and am barren, an
exile and driven out, and who hath brought
up these, behold I was left alone, these, where
were they ?"

This passage seems to represent ancient
Israel as soliloquising, saying, Who hath begotten for me even these, seeing I have lost my
children and am barren, an exile and driven
out, a cast-off family, and who hath brought
up these—these Christians, children of Shem,
Ham and Japheth? Behold I was left alone,
but these where were they, and whence came
they—this great nationality of Israel restored,
greater in numbers, greater in power, and
greater in learning, more progressive and
aggressive than all the children that I have

lost? They claim to be, and are, leaders of
the world in thought, in invention, in civil and
religious liberty, in all the higher graces of
Christian life; "who hath brought up these,"
and whence came they? "Refrain thy voice
from weeping and thine eyes from tears, . . .
there is hope in thine end, saith the Lord, that
children, [*i. e.*, spiritual children of Abraham
or Christians,] shall come again to their own
border," in the day of their great restoration.
Jer. xxxi: 16, 17. "For if the casting away
of them [of Ancient Israel] be the reconciling
of the world, what shall the receiving [of
Israel restored] be but life from the dead?"
Rom. xi: 15—life to the dead nations by the
purifying, exalting and saving power of the
Gospel. The influence of the government of ✓
Israel restored, will be life to the land of dead
monarchies and autocracies. Their people
will rise up and shake off the grave-clothes of
despotism and start on higher planes of development. And in this manner the nations will✓
"receive life from the dead."

V. 22. "Thus saith the Lord Jehovah, Behold I will lift up to the nations my hand,
and I will set up my banner to the peoples,

and they will bring thy sons in their arms
and thy daughters shall be carried on their
shoulders." The Lord is here represented as
beckoning with his hand to the nations, and
as setting up his banner to the peoples, sum-
moning them to start on the great migration
to their promised land. Their sons should be
carried in their arms, and their daughters on
their shoulders. They would not wait for
expensive preparation: but as soon as God
would point out the way and their duty, they
would leave all and start as promptly as possible, following the banner of His providence,
and the pointing of His hand. Has this prophecy not been fully realized in the discovery
of America and in the movement of the multitudes from the nations to this country?
The discovery of America was the "banner
lifted up" to attract the attention of the
nations and people, while its vast resources,
with its social, civil and religious privileges,
was "the hand" of God that pointed them
hither.

V. 23. "And kings shall be thy nursing
fathers and their queens thy nursing mothers;
face to the ground shall they bow to thee and

they shall lick the dust of thy feet, and thou shalt know that I am Jehovah, whose waiters [*i. e.*, those who wait for His help] shall not be ashamed."

.This prophecy is now our history. Did not the kings and queens of Europe encourage colonization in America for near two centuries, by their money, by grants of land, by charters, and in various ways? It was an immense undertaking. It required brave hearts, strong arms, and the wealth of kings and queens to support and maintain the early colonization of our country. And so it became the pet scheme of royalty to colonize and settle this land. This was God's plan to establish Japheth on these shores, to plant the Church here and to roll back the heathen tribes that occupied the territory. A multitude of names in our country will forever remind us that kings were our nursing fathers and their queens were our nursing mothers. Maryland, Virginia, Carolina and Georgia, among the old thirteen States, and King William, Prince George, Prince Edward, Queen Anne and dozens more counties will forever bear testimony to the fulfillment of this prophecy. As time rolls on, and as God's eternal plans are unfolded in providence as they are in prophecy, the latter part of this verse will be as literally and as astonishingly fulfilled. "And thou shalt know that I am Jehovah, whose waiters shall not be ashamed." They are not ashamed; and they even now see, in part, what wonderful things He has done; and they confidently "wait" for the rest to be hastened in its time.

V. 24. "Shall the prey be taken from the mighty, and shall the captivity of the righteous be delivered?" As the hawk swoops down upon the dove and feeds upon the helpless, so have popes and priests and merciless tyrants preyed upon the humble followers of Christ, and the captivity of the righteous has been drawn out through many centuries of blood and torture. But now, thank God, there is a land whose Constitution guarantees freedom and the full enjoyment of all religious privileges to His people. Thank God, the prey has been taken from the mighty, and the captivity of the righteous is ended. America is not only "the land of the free and the home of the brave," but the, heaven-appointed place of Israel's freedom, deliverance from oppression and restoration.

V. 25. "For thus saith Jehovah, also the captives of the mighty shall be taken and the prey of the terrible shall be delivered, and with thy adversaries I will contend and I will save thy sons."

And has the Lord not contended with our adversaries and overthrown them? And has He not established this great providential government, to which His people may flee, and have fled by scores of thousands? And here He hath "saved his sons," saved His people from the rack, from torture and despotism, and hath furnished them a home, where God alone is King. Truly "the Lord shall comfort Zion, he will comfort all her waste places and he will make her wilderness like Eden and her desert like the garden of the Lord; joy and gladness shall be found therein, thanksgiving and the voice of melody." Isa. li: 4. Strange that this wonderful prophecy, and still more wonderful fulfillment have not been understood by the Church. Strange that this long-spread feast of heavenly love has never been uncovered before. It furnishes bread to strengthen and wine to cheer. Let it be read from the mountain tops. Let it be heralded from shore to shore. Let the nations know that "the Lord is Jehovah whose waiters shall not be ashamed."

V. 26. "And I will make thine oppressors eat their own flesh, and, as with new wine, they shall be drunken with their own blood."

I take this to be a metaphorical expression to show the deep chagrin and drunken rage of oppressors or tyrants, when they have lost their prey and when they have lost large territory and dominion. It was a bitter pill for England to give up all right and title to the United States, and to acknowledge our independence and nationality. After more than an hundred years, she has hardly forgiven us yet. But she could not help herself. It was the Lord's own doing for the glory of His Church, and for a blessing to this sin-cursed world, that "all flesh shall know that I Jehovah am thy Savior and thy Redeemer, the Mighty One of Jacob." The covenant-keeping God is Israel's God, and He will make all His promises true.

"Praise ye the Lord. Praise Him for His mighty acts: praise Him according to His excellent greatness. Let everything that hath breath praise the Lord. Praise ye the Lord."

CHAPTER VIII.

SETTING UP OF ISRAEL

"The Second Time."—Isa xi. 10–16.

THE first part of this chapter relates to the coming of Messiah, to the righteousness of the Gospel, to its peaceable conquests and wonderful moral transformations. The prophet here seems to give a general view of Messiah's reign, calling attention to grand results rather than to the means of their accomplishment. The idea of His spiritual reign in and over the children of men is mainly intended. But in the latter part of this chapter, the prophet describes another development of the Rod of Jesse more definitely and concisely. As Messiah, or the Lord's Anointed, ruled in ancient Israel, so Christ, or His Anointed, rules in the New Testament Israel, the same Lord over both dispensations. The Church of God was " Is-√

rael," and is "Israel," the same in ancient as
in modern times. The Church under this dispensation is marked by an enlarged development and change of dress. In the ancient
economy, one family was developed in types
and symbols, both as to the true religion and
the true government, giving ample instruction
in every department symbolically. In the
new economy, we have, or are to have, the
realization of this divine religion in all the
families of earth. In ancient Israel, in the
days of the Judges, there was a divinely appointed theocratic-republican government, as
a beautiful symbol. In the new economy, we
must look for its realization in grander proportions, in the setting up of Israel "the
second time." As the religion of ancient Israel
is to be developed into the world-wide religion
of the new economy, so the symbolic, theocratic-republican government of ancient Israel
is to be realized in the government of Israel
restored, under the world-embracing Christian
dispensation. As ancient Israel had a place
on the earth assigned it, with metes and
bounds, in which territory it accomplished its
symbolic mission, so Israel restored has a

place on the earth assigned to it, though vastly larger, with metes and bounds, in which it is to begin its work of restoration: but its mission, unlike ancient Israel's, is to expand and enlarge, until it embraces all nations. The "Stone" is to grow larger and larger, until "it fills the whole earth," until "the thrones shall be cast down," until monarchy and despotism are crushed and "driven away like chaff from the summer threshing-floors," and the world shall be blessed with truth and the largest share of civil and religious freedom.

V. 10. "In that day, the sprout of Jesse, which is to stand up, shall be a signal to the peoples: unto it the nations shall tread—[go] —and his place of rest shall be (*cavodth*) abundance." "In that day"—in the day of the triumphs of the Gospel, "in the time of the end" "when the power of the holy people shall cease to be scattered," when the "Stone shall be cut out of the mountain without hands," when "the ancient of days came, and judgment was given to the saints of the Most High, in that day "the sprout of Jesse" shall be set up.

"The Rod of Jesse" is different from "the

Sprout of Jesse." The words are different. Separate and distinct words are employed to convey separate and distinct ideas; and the objects spoken of are different. " The Rod of Jesse " refers to Christ in the Church ; but " the Sprout of Jesse " refers to Christ in Israel restored. This we learn from the subsequent description. There are two potent reasons why Israel "set up the second time " should be termed "the Sprout of Jesse." 1st. Jesse lived in the last days of the divinely appointed government of the Judges. In his day the government was changed from Judges to Kings, against the divine protest. Jesse stands as a representative of theocratic republicanism. 2nd. Jesse also stands as a representative of political power. For from him came David and Solomon, the two most powerful kings of Israel. Thus "the Sprout of Jesse " is a most befitting symbol of the divinely chosen system of government, clothed with political power. This "Sprout is to stand up as a signal to the peoples, and to it the nations shall tread "—or go. This famous signal to which the nations are "to seek," " to go," " to come," " to assemble," is the government of Israel set up " the second time," or the United States of America, as has been demonstrated by a number of prophecies fulfilled.

"And his place of rest—or residence—shall be (*cavodth*) abundance." This describes the land of Israel's restoration—large, abundant in wealth and resources of all sorts, and accessible to the commerce of the world, for the nations shall go thither.

" Shall be a signal to the peoples." Our government is different from all other governments on the earth. The religion of the Bible is its corner-stone, the Church and State, like twins, are separate and distinct, yet each is bound to the other by the strongest cords and tenderest ties. Their mutual strength is increased by their mutual growth. Like good neighbors, they each attend to their own affairs, without either intermeddling with the other's rights. Here, no one lords it over God's heritage. Here, our constitution requires us to render unto Cæsar the things that are Cæsar's and unto God the things that are God's. Here, a generous soil yields abundantly to honest toil. Hence, truthfully, it is called the land of " abundance." Here, every man is free. Here, the humblest citizen may be promoted to the highest offices of honor and trust. To such a " signal " it is no wonder the nations come. " It is the Lord's doing, and it is marvelous in our eyes."

V. 11. "And it shall be in that day, the Lord shall add His hand a second time, to set upright the remainder of His people which shall be left, from Assyria, and from Egypt, and from Pathros, and from Cush, and from Elam, and from Shinar, and from Hamath, and from the islands of the sea."

"And it shall be in that day"—at the time appointed, at the end of the woman's sojourn in the wilderness, at the end of the 1,260 symbolic years, " the Lord shall add his hand a second time to set up the remainder of His people." The first time the Lord "set up " " His people " in a national capacity was in the Promised Land, after they were brought out of Egypt. He divided unto them the land according to the thirteen tribes. He gave to each tribe its portion. There they lived through long centuries, in prosperity and in adversity, until their times had been filled.

Then "the sceptre departed from Judah," and then they were hopelessly scattered to the ends of the earth, as unwilling monuments of the truthfulness of God's Word. For more than eighteen centuries they have been wandering as exiles and strangers in strange lands, and must still wander on "until the fullness of the Gentiles be come in." In the meantime, Israel will be restored—not the Jews —not the carnal seed of Abraham: no, no; they do not now constitute Israel; but those who believe in the Lord Jesus Christ and are born of the Spirit—these constitute the true spiritual Israel. "If ye are Christ's, then are ye Abraham's seed and heirs according to the promise." It is this spiritual, believing Israel, which will be restored to a second nationality, in all the grandeur programmed by the prophets, even in this land, which God has promised and given to them. It is this Christian Israel which is to revolutionize the nations and bring them back to the control of King Jesus. This is the glorious destiny of the Church, working in, through, and with the fifth nationality, as its great co-worker, in the complete restoration of Israel, when "the

thrones shall be cast down" and Jesus shall
be "Lord of all," king of nations as He is
now king of saints. This is what is meant by
Israel restored, and not the return of the Jews
to Palestine. It is sad to see whole volumes
of learned ignorance on this subject. Let the
sad fact be remembered that the Jews, as a
people, are not Israel at all; for they cast off
Jesus, their Messiah, and He cast them off.
As the great Apostle tells us, "because of un-
belief they were broken off." The true Israel
of God, in all ages, are those who love and
fear Him, and who walk in His ways, whether
they be Jews or Gentiles. The Israel under
the Jewish economy, has had its day and it
is past. The next development is still the
Israel of God, under the Christian dispensation, on a world-embracing plan.

As the "Stone" was small at first, with a
definite location, and ultimately filled the
whole earth; so Israel set up the second time,
must be expected to have a definite location,
with boundaries well marked. These boundaries had been found, and definitely described, in the field-notes of Ezekiel, the inspired surveyor. Also Isaiah, and Daniel,

and John, all point with astonishing directness
to the United States, as the chosen territory
where the Lord should "add His hand a
second time, to set up, erect, or establish the
remainder of His people, which shall be left
from Assyria, and from Egypt, and from Pathros, and from Cush, and from Elam, and from
Shinar, and from Hamath, and from the islands
of the sea."

These countries are all put metonymically
for the countries into which Christians have
been driven, and from which they come, and
are to come, to the land of their restoration.
Because the nations mentioned in this verse
have long ceased to exist, and have passed
away.

"And from the islands of the sea." Addison
Alexander says, this does not mean "merely
islands in the strict sense, but the shores of
the Mediterranean, whether insular or continental, and substantially equivalent to Europe,
and here put last, as being the most import-
ant." And is it not an historical fact that the
first settlers of our country, and the founders
of our government, came from England and
Scotland, and Ireland—literally "from the

islands of the sea"? And since then multitudes have come from all parts of Europe, and of the world. The word translated "left" from Assyria, etc., is very expressive, it is (*sha-ar*), and means "left over," or that which "remains;" implying that there was no room for them in those countries, that they were crowded out by opposing forces, by oppression, or persecution. This interpretation is fully confirmed by the next verse.

V. 12. "And he shall set up a signal for the nations and assemble the outcasts of Israel, [or those thrust out of Israel] and the dispersed of Judah shall gather together from the four corners of the earth." The "signal set up for the nations," was the setting up of the Stone Government, or fifth nationality. It would be a safe retreat for all the persecuted for Christ's sake. It would become so famous a retreat for the "worn-out saints," that it would appear as "a signal for the nations" of the oppressed, where the outcasts of Israel and the scattered of Judah should gather together. Israel and Judah are Hebrew names for the people of God, and mean the thrust-out or exiled: scattered Christians should be gathered in this "place of rest, in Israel a second time set up," from the four corners of the earth." And has not this prophecy been literally fulfilled ? It and its fulfillment stand to-day as a signal to the nations of the truthfulness and of the divine inspiration of God's Word, showing, as clear as the sun in the heavens, that His prophecy and providence move along, side by side, through the ages. At the same time, they are two living and uncorruptible witnesses for God and for His truth, before the sinful and God-forgetting generations.

"Shall gather together from the four corners of the earth." Are they not and have they not been, coming to this country from every nationality ? There is no other nation on earth that has risen like it. Its time and place and circumstances all fill and fit the divine photograph of prophecy, just as the shadow fits the substance. Whether men will see it, or close their eyes against it, the truth will stand forever the same. God's Word is an infinite store-house, filled with rich provisions for the saints. But alas, how many will not partake of its bounties! They are poor,

lean and starving. They say " our soul loath-
eth this light bread." All such had better
watch out for " the fiery-flying serpents."
For the Lord hath spoken. And " he that
hath ears to hear, let him hear."

V. 13. "And the envy of Ephraim shall
depart, and the adversaries of Judah shall be
cut off: Ephraim shall not envy Judah, and
Judah shall not vex [press upon] Ephraim."
The entire abolition of the old grudge between
Ephraim and Judah, is used metonymically
to show the harmony which will exist between
all Christians in Israel restored, or " in the
place of his rest." Addison Alexander says :
" That this prophecy was not fulfilled in the
return from exile, is sufficiently notorious.
That it had not been fulfilled when Christ
came, is plain from the continued enmity
between the Jews, Samaritans and Galileans.
The only fulfillment it has ever had, is in the
the abolition of all national and sectional dis-
tinctions in the Christian Church, to which
converted Jews as well as others must submit." But the prophet is here speaking
about " the sprout of Jesse,"—about when " He
shall set up a signal for the nations," when

" the Lord shall add His hand a second time to set up the remainder of His people." He is speaking about the times in Israel restored. Then all national and sectional jealousy shall be done away, when all peoples shall gather round the cross. There will be different denominations at that time, but they will form the different parts of that grand anthem of praise, saying " Unto him that loved us and washed us from our sins in His own blood and hath made us kings and priests unto God and His Father, to Him be glory and dominion forever and ever. Amen."

V. 14. "And they shall fly upon the shoulders of the Philistines towards the west; together they shall spoil the sons of the east, and they shall lay their hand upon Edom and Moab and the children of Ammon shall obey them." It has been customary for many commentators to translate the verb *huph* in this verse, " to fly" as an eagle flies upon its prey, making Ephraim and Judah fly upon the Philistines as their prey. But this translation is not supported by the sense or by Scripture precedent. This word simply means " to fly" without any " prey" connected with

it, as birds fly. See Job. v: 7. Prov. xxiii:
5. Deut. iv: 17: also, of locusts flying. Nah.
iii: 17, etc., conveying the idea of rapid locomotion. Ephraim and Judah stand metonymically for Christian people "in the latter
days." The Philistines represent the people
of "the islands of the sea," or western
Europe. "Upon the shoulder," is the place
where burdens are carried.

Now let us read this verse with common
sense interpretation. "And at that time,"
when the Lord would "set His hand a second
time" to restore His people, they shall be
carried on ships, for this is the only means of
transportation across the ocean, and must be
the meaning of that symbolic expression,
"borne on the shoulders of the Philistines
towards the west," to America, to the United
States, to the place of His rest that is
"abundance." Truly the Philistines [Western
Europe] have mightily assisted in gathering
together His people to this land of the second
setting up of Israel. I cannot see how any
sense can be made out of this passage, with
any other interpretation. With this interpretation, it is all clear. It is in accordance with

the right meaning of words, and with the
facts in the case. Did not our persecuted
forefathers, who were the outcasts of Israel
and the scattered of Judah, did they not come
in ships from Western Europe, or " on the
shoulders of the Philistines towards the west,"
and first people the eastern coast of the
United States and set up this government,
which is to-day, and has been for an hundred
years, " a signal to the persecuted of the
nations "?   And are not " the peoples " fleeing
to our shores from the nations of Europe, by
hundreds of thousands every year? This
prophecy must mean our country.   It can't
refer to old Palestine, for then they would
have to fly to the east, instead of the west,
and thereby reverse the whole order of the
prophecy. How simple! How plain and
easy to be understood is God's Word when
rightly interpreted!   We should humbly
search the Scriptures to find out what the
Lord hath said, and not dictate to Him what
He ought to have said.

"Together they shall spoil the sons of the
east; they shall lay their hand upon Edom
and Moab, and the children of Ammon shall
obey them."

The peoples mentioned here have passed away, and are all dead thousands of years ago. So it is perfectly clear this prophecy does not refer to those dead nations. But as Edom and Moab and Ammon and the children of the East were enemies to the progress and prosperity of Ephraim and Judah; and as Ephraim and Judah were promised that they should conquer and bring into obedience their enemies, so by metonymy the Christian Israel, ✓ "set up a second time," in the fifth nationality, would "in the latter days," as "the Stone," crush and utterly destroy all of monarchy and autocracy; and as the ancient of days would "cast down the thrones," in like manner all Israel, united under the fostering care of a free republican government, will overthrow and subdue Edom, Moab, Ammon, or all powers opposing the growth, expansion and universal dominion of civil and religious liberty and the world-wide extension of human freedom. These enemies to the highest attainments of human excellence, under the gospel dispensation "in the latter days," are to be utterly overthrown, destroyed and scattered to the winds like

chaff from the summer threshing floors, so that
no place shall be found for them.   The nations
must submit to, and obey, the government of
the king of nations.   Such seems to be the
programme marked out in this prophecy of
the triumphs of the Church under the reign of
King Immanuel.

V. 15. "And Jehovah will utterly destroy
the tongue of the Egyptian sea; and shake
his hand upon the river in the strength of his
wind, and smite it in the seven streams and
cause his people to tread it in shoes" [or, pass
over dry shod.]

V. 16. "And there shall be a highway for
the remainder of my people, which shall be
left from Assyria, as there was for Israel, in
the day of his coming up from the land of
Egypt."

These two verses are retrospective and
prospective: and tell how these wonderful results are and were brought about.   The
"tongue of the Egyptian Sea," or Red Sea,
was the first great difficulty that the children
of Israel met on their way to the Promised
Land.   It is prophesied that this difficulty
shall be utterly destroyed, and shall be no

obstacle to the march of the Lord's people, in the great restoration. In the providence of God, has not the Red Sea been converted into a great highway for the nations? By the opening of the Suez Canal, "the tongue of the Egyptian Sea" has been utterly destroyed as a difficulty or obstacle; it opens a way several thousand miles the shortest and best from Europe to India and to all seaports of Asia. Thus the facilities for travel have been greatly increased, thereby bringing the ends of the earth nearer together. So that "the children of the east," as well as "the Philistines" of the west, may see the "Sprout of Jesse" set up as an "ensign for the nations," and "the outcasts of Israel" may be "gathered together from the four corners of the earth," "to the place of his rest," or place of his residence.

"And shake his hand [in a threatening manner] upon the river, in the strength of his wind [as much as to say, 'you will not always be a terror and a hindrance,'] and will smite it in seven streams and cause his people to pass over dry shod." I am not sure that we should confine "the tongue of the Egyptian

Sea," to the Red Sea, or " the river to be smitten in seven streams" to the Euphrates.
These famous obstacles to migration, in ancient times, I think are here mentioned metonymically for all great difficulties and obstacles to migration that must and will be over-
come by improved modes of locomotion: such
as steamboats, steamships, and railroads that
now laugh at difficulties. What once were
regarded as impossible barriers to travel, are
now passed over like a bird on the wing.
Oceans and seas, instead of separating
nations, are now great highways by which
they are brought nearer together. And as
for rivers being difficulties, they are now
crossed in cars on our great highways, as if
they were not there. Thus the prophecy is
fulfilled, because the deep water obstacles of
former times are now "utterly destroyed,"
and the many thousands that migrate in these
times may " pass over dry shod."

"And there shall be a highway for the
remainder of my people which shall be left
from Assyria." Assyria of course has passed
away thousands of years ago; but the name
is used here to represent those countries from

which the Lord's people shall be gathered.
As His miraculous providence opened a way
through the Red Sea for His ancient people,
so His wonderful providence has opened a
highway of travel for His people to gather
themselves together into "the place of His
rest," or place of His residence. As ancient
Israel offered thanksgiving and praise on the
other side of the sea, for their escape and
deliverance from Egypt, so our fathers in this
land of Israel's restoration, have often offered
thanks, and sung hymns of praise, for their
deliverance from tyranny, oppression and
persecution. After ages of wrongs and exile
and martyrdom, they were permitted to enter
their own land of liberty and "abundance,
with hearts overflowing with gratitude. They
shouted His praise for their wonderful deliverance. Their song was written in prophecy
2,500 years ago. And when the appointed
time came—when Israel was delivered and
restored—there was a people prepared and
ready to sing the song of deliverance. And
they shouted it with their lips from overflowing hearts, saying, "O Lord, I will praise
Thee; though Thou wast angry with me,

Thine anger is turned away and thou comfortedst me. Behold, God is my salvation; I will trust and not be afraid; for the Lord Jehovah is my strength and my song; he also is become my salvation. Sing unto the Lord, for He hath done excellent things; this is known in all the earth. Cry out and shout, thou inhabitant of Zion; for great is the Holy One of Israel in the midst of thee."

The coincidences in this prophecy with the United States are many and remarkable.

1st. "The Sprout of Jesse," which is the "signal to the peoples" that was to be "set up," corresponds to the setting up of this government on a Christian basis.

2nd. "Unto it the nations shall tread." And have "the peoples" not come hither to these States "from the four corners of the earth"?

3rd. "The place of his rest shall be *abundance.*" And is not this a land of abundance—abundance of everything? There is no country like it. No other word could have described it so well.

4th. "The second setting up of Israel" literally coincides with the "setting up" of this government, chronologically, geographically and prophetically.

5th. " The outcasts of Israel, or persecuted Christians, were to come to their "place of rest." And did not the persecuted Huguenots, Quakers, Covenanters, Pilgrims, and multitudes of oppressed Christians find " a place of rest," or residence in this land?

6th. They, " the peoples," should come to this land " from the four corners of the earth." And has not this prophecy been fulfilled to the letter?

7th. "And they shall fly upon the shoulders of the Philistines towards the west." And did not Europe, and particularly Western Europe, or " the islands of the sea," send the great multitude of the early settlers to this country? And the cry is, " still they come," daily by thousands.

8th. "And Jehovah shall utterly destroy the tongue of the Egyptian sea." And has not the utter destruction of the difficulties and hindrances to migration taken place at the time appointed, and in the right manner? We behold the fulfillment of this prophecy in the increased powers of locomotion and facilities for transportation. All this has been done since the setting up of the Stone kingdom, and has greatly conduced to its development and prosperity.

9th. "And there shall be a highway for the remainder of my people" to come to "the land of their rest," or residence. This prophecy is partly fulfilled, in the modern improvements in travel, both on land and sea, and also in the civil and religious liberty of our people. All may come, who please.

10th. The song of thanksgiving and praise for deliverance, which closes this prophecy, has met a wonderful coincidence in the gratitude and songs of praise, sung by our fore· fathers for their great victory and deliverance from tyranny and oppression, and for *their own land!* of liberty and abundance.

These are some of the remarkable points of coincidence of these prophecies in our country. The shadow fits the substance. Other points in this prophecy, "in their *time*," will be even more astonishing in their coincidence than those that are now history. The providences of God are on their grand, ceaseless, onward march, to accomplish, and now are daily accomplishing, the fulfillment of ancient prophecies — the ancient programme of the nations and of the Church — with astonishing exactness. Let all the world behold with wonder, and know that "the Lord God Omnipotent reigneth."

CHAPTER IX.

THE ANCIENT OF DAYS.

A Symbol of Israel Restored.—*Daniel vii. 9-27.*

"I BEHELD till the thrones were cast down, and the ancient of days did sit, whose garment was white as snow, and the hair of his head like the pure wool: his throne was like the fiery flame, and his wheels as burning fire. A fiery stream issued and came forth from before him; thousand thousands ministered unto him, and ten thousand times ten thousand stood before him: the judgment was set, and the books were opened."

We now approach a subject of more than ordinary difficulty, because its true meaning is enveloped in such gorgeous drapery. Who is the ancient of days? This is the first question to be answered. Many commentators and poets have attributed this name to the first person of the adorable Trinity—to God, the Father. But this opinion cannot be correct, for five reasons—

1st. Because God the Father is nowhere represented in the Scriptures as incarnate, or having bodily shape.

2nd. Because "the Father judgeth no man; but hath committed all judgment unto the Son." (John v : 22.)

3rd. Because God the Father is the ancient of eternity, and not the ancient of days. He is without beginning of days or end of years.

4th. Because Daniel's interpretation is very explicit. He says : " these great beasts, which are four, are four kings [or kingdoms] which shall arise out of the earth. But the saints of the Most High shall take the kingdom, and possess the kingdom, forever, even forever and ever.'" So the flaming chariot throne of the ancient of days represents the conquering government of the saints—the fifth great nationality of earth, clothed with political power.

5th. Because "the judgment shall sit, and THEY shall take away his dominion." *They*, the government of the saints, " shall take away " the dominion of " the little horn " which " spake great words against the Most High," and " wore out the saints of the Most High." " *They* "—the saints, the friends of civil and religious liberty, " shall take away his dominion, to consume and to destroy it unto the end."

As " the Stone cut out of the mountain without hands," that crushed the image of monarchy, represents a new kingdom, the fifth great government of earth, which was to arise after the other four kingdoms, and to conquer all nations, and to continue until the end of time ; so the kingdom of " the ancient of days," another symbol of the fifth government, was to arise and rule after the four kingdoms had passed away, which Daniel saw in his vision of the " four beasts." As the Stone government arose entirely outside of the limits of the Roman Empire, so the kingdom of the " ancient of days " was to rise outside of those limits also : for it is the same fifth government, in a different vision, with some additional revelations. Both of these symbols are synchronal, and point forward to the universal dominion of Christianity, under a pure civil government.

The judgment scene, at which the "ancient of days" presides, is described in glowing colors, because of the grandeur of the occasion. The majesty of the Most High had been insulted, and must be avenged, as well as the wrongs and injuries of the saints, whom "'the little horn' thought to wear out." His garment was white as snow, and his hair "like the pure wool," emblematic of purity. His ermine of judicial authority was of spotless whiteness. His chariot-throne of flaming fire, signified that nothing but truth and eternal right could stand before it. All the chaff and tinsel, as well as the cruel wrongs of monarchy, and monarchy itself as essentially evil, will be consumed and destroyed together unto the end.

"A fiery stream issued, and came forth from before him." A stream of influence, a stream of prosperity and happiness among the masses, a stream of human liberty, also a stream of periodicals, books, and literature of various kinds that kindle in the soul a fiery love of freedom ; also streams of light and truth—all, all issuing from the government of "the ancient of days," and constantly diffused among

the millions of monarchy, is like fire to
kindle revolution, to overthrow, and burn
up the foundations of absolutism. This
"fiery stream" wakes up the slumbering
millions, produces a state of unrest, and a
desire for independence and human progress.
For an hundred years this "fiery stream"
has been flowing with an increasing swell,
and behold what effects! What wonderful
results have already been produced! And
still this "fiery stream" is constantly swell-
ing with our increasing prosperity, now flowing like a flood, soon to accomplish its divine
mission of revolution, overthrow, and destruction of civil and religious bondage and despotism. The hand of Providence is directing
all these things to the accomplishment of His
eternal plans.

There is a deep significance in the expression "The ancient of days did sit." Away
back in the ages, there was a little Republi-
can-Democratic theocracy, in the days of the
Judges of ancient Israel, when the people
chose their own rulers under the divine direction: it was so small, and comparatively
short-lived, and so far in advance of the

times, that it produced no commotion among
the surrounding despotisms. It felt lonely
and despised. But it was a great fact. It
was pure seed, planted deep in the pages of
eternal truth. The people were happy and
prosperous under their government, and the
Lord was their King. That government served
its purpose as a splendid type, and passed
away. Its history was written, and is now
read by millions. It lived just long enough
to show to the nations what had been, what
should be, what could be, and what would be
accomplished in God's own time, under the
transforming world-wide Christian dispensation. And so it came to pass, when "the
time of the end" had come, when "the power
of the holy people had ceased to be scattered"—when the 1,260 symbolic days were
ended, after "the taking away of the daily
sacrifice," when "the time, times and an
half" of the woman's sojourn in the wilderness were ended; then the Stone Kingdom
was set up; then the ancient of days came,
exactly at the time appointed, and was re-
established on a scale, the grandeur of which
is adequate to the necessities of its wonderful

mission; then justice was rendered to the saints of the Most High; "and the time came that the saints possessed the kingdom," or dominion. America, so long hid, was discovered, the United States government was established, and "a nation was born in a day." Now we are living in the land of Israel restored, under the re-establishment of the government of "the ancient of days," in the fifth nationality, the last and noblest form of government the world will have; where men and mind are free from the tyranny of superstition, and free from political slavery; for "the saints of the Most High shall take the kingdom, and possess the kingdom forever, even forever and ever." Blessed truth, cheering hope, as the promised day dawns into a glorious reality. As the ever-widening circles of the government of "the ancient of days" extend from point to point, in its ceaseless march of conquest, diffusing light and truth, liberty of soul and true manliness, it leaves forever the history of the past to tell its sad story of oppression and wrongs—the dark and bloody history of almost 6,000 years, filled with the wrecks of human greatness, with tears and blighted hopes, while the groans and sighs of uncounted millions made the sad and doleful monotone of the passing generations. All this, and infinitely more, makes up,the dark background, upon which the increasingly glorious government of " the ancient of days " is,to shine with greater and greater light, even with an heavenly splendor. This sounds like ✓ swollen language, but it falls far below the predicted reality.

Another remarkable statement is here made : when " the ancient of days did sit," when he first came to his seat, " thousand, thousands," ministered unto him ; that is, three " thousands," as there were three " times." Now if we multiply 1,000×1,000 we have 1,000,000 ; then, " thousands " is equal to two more "thousand," multiplied in like manner ; then, by adding the results, we have just 3,000,000, the number " that ministered unto him." This was the number that went with Moses from ✓ Egypt to Palestine, as near as can be counted, when ancient Israel was first set up as a nation, or with an independent government of their own. In like manner, after more than 3,600 years, it was also the number of the ✓

inhabitants of the United States, when our government was first set up, and declared independent, in 1776, when Israel's restoration was begun. As Joshua led his three millions into the land of promise, and gave them liberty, and a country for their home and for their development, in like manner, Washington led his three millions from political slavery into a land of liberty—which was also a land of prophecy and of providence—for their own country, and for their children's children, to the latest generation; for "the saints," *i. e.*, the friends of civil and religious liberty, "shall possess the kingdom forever, even forever and ever," or through the ages.

Daniel said, "I saw in my vision by night, and behold the four winds of the heaven strove upon the great sea" of the nations and peoples. "And four great beasts came up from the sea, diverse one from another. The first was like a lion;" this represented the Babylonian Empire, which culminated in the reign of Nebuchadnezzar. The second was "like to a bear"; this symbolized the Medo-Persian Empire, which culminated in the reign of Cyrus. The third was like a

leopard": this was a symbol of the Macedonian
Empire, which culminated in the reign of Alexander the Great. The "fourth beast was
dreadful and terrible, and strong exceedingly;
and it had great iron teeth . . . it was diverse from all the beasts that were before it;
and it had ten horns." "And another little horn
came up, before whom there were three of the
first horns plucked up by the roots; and behold, in this horn were eyes like the eyes of
man, and a mouth speaking great things."
. . . "And he shall speak great words
against the Most High, and shall wear out the
saints of the Most High, and think to change
times and laws : and they [the saints] shall
be given into his hand, until a time, times,
and the dividing of a time." The "fourth
beast," all commentators agree, was the Roman Empire, which culminated in the reign
of the Cæsars. The "ten horns" represented
the ten kingdoms that rose up after the Roman
monarchy and occupied the same territory.
And the "little horn" that rose up, "before
whom three" of the first horns "fell," represents the illegitimate union of Church and
State, that developed into the Papacy. This

politico-ecclesiastical concubinage brought
forth a terrible progeny. They spake blas-
phemous words against the Most High. They
persecuted, imprisoned, and martyred the
saints by millions. Their hellish purpose was
to "wear them out." For more than a thousand years, the history of this "little horn"
is stained with innocent blood, and filled with
loathsome dungeons, and all sorts of devilish
torture. Its choice music was the groans of
dying Christians, their wailings on the rack,
and their lamentations in prison; and the
tears and sobs of heart-broken saints, wandering as exiles and homeless in strange lands,
afforded fiendish delight. But let God be
praised forever, because He is true to His
promises. At the end of the 1,260 symbolic
years, exactly at the time appointed, "the
ancient of days came," and justice was rendered to the saints of the Most High; govern-
mental authority and a great country were
given to His people, where the horns of monarchy can never hurt them any more, and
where the "little horn," all gory with the
blood of saints, can never touch them
again.

The Constitution and laws of the United States are founded on the Bible, and on the principles of equity and "everlasting right-eousness," reminding us again that our government is "the ancient of days," or the "stone cut out of the mountain" of Christi-anity. Here all Christians can feel at home, for it *is* their home, and their land, reserved in God's providence for this purpose, and for these times. So that from henceforth, under the ægis of this government, the Church may unfurl her banners for the conquest of the world, in accordance with the divine pro-gramme, and no horns of monarchy, or of the devil, can gore them any more, and no one dare disturb them any more, or make them afraid in their worship of the Lord of Hosts.

In order to remove all doubt about the truthfulness of our interpretation of "the an-cient of days," we have shown that it is only another symbol for "the Stone kingdom,"— that it is "Israel restored," that it is the fifth nationality—that it is, and is being realized, in the United States of America. Now to demonstrate the truthfulness and correctness of the interpretation, the very *time* is speci-

fied when "the ancient of days" should
come. It is written in the 25th verse of this
chapter. "And they," the saints, or friends
of civil and religious liberty, "shall be given
into his hand"—the hand of "the little horn,"
"until a time, and times, and the dividing of
a time," that is, for three and an half times,
or 1,260 symbolic years. Now at what time
was the Church (or the saints) given into the
hands of the little horn ; or when were Church
and State first united ? From history we learn
that Constantine the Great was made head of
the Church, or the Church was placed under
political control, at the Council of Nice, in
Bithynia, about June 17th, A. D. 325. Now
let us count from that Council—from the day
when political power was given to the Church,
3½ "times," or 1,260 symbolic years—of cut-
off, or *shortened time:* remember that this is
the "key" to the "times" of the prophets.
Since 360 always represents a prophetic year,
it may represent a year of 364 parts. Then
364 multiplied by 364 is equal to 132,496 : to
which add ¼, or sabbatic time, and we have
151,424. And since 360 is contained in 1,260,
just 3½ times ; then 3½ times one "*time*," or

151,424, is equal to 529,984 days, in solar time; or 1,451 years and 17 days—the time that the saints were given into the power of " the little horn." Now add this 1,451 years and 17 days, to June 17th, A. D. 325, and it gives us exactly 1,776, July the 4th, the year and the day, that the United States were declared independent, and the time exactly when " a nation was born in a day," when " the ancient of days came," and established his dominion. This calculation is astonishing, and its truthfulness is startling. The glory of ancient Israel, under a Republican theocracy, has been restored and re-established, on a vastly grander scale than in the days of the Judges. " The ancient of days " has come, and is in the strength and beauty of his youthful manhood; his dominion has been set up in the United States. But his work has only begun, in comparison with the grandeur of his mission. We stand at the beginning; the end is far in the future. In this little book we only speak of facts—of things that have been, or that now are. We deal not with vague theories and unproved hypotheses, but with eternal truth and solid, substantial facts.

Of the unfulfilled prophecies, in the inspired programme of "the ancient of days" of his universal conquests, and establishment of righteousness among the nations, we will not speak. That must be left to the future historian and commentator. How these glorious triumphs will be brought about, God knows, and that is enough. He will see that the whole programme will be perfectly fulfilled. Let God be praised, we have seen the beginning. It is sufficient for us to know, as we stand at the threshold of promised glory to the Church and to the nations, "that the saints of the Most High shall take the kingdom, and possess dominion forever, even forever and ever." It is legitimate for us to close this chapter by quoting the divine programme, in which we catch a glimpse of what are to be the grand results which are yet far in the future, verses 26 and 27. "The judges were seated to take away his dominion," *i. e.*, of "the little horn"—or ecclesiastical and State domination—"to consume and to destroy it unto the end. And kingdom and dominion, and the greatness of the kingdom, under the whole heaven, shall be given to the people of the saints of the Most High, whose kingdom is an everlasting kingdom, and all dominions shall serve and obey Him." This is the Lord's doing; what He has done; and what is yet to be done.

Truly "it is marvelous in our eyes." Monarchs and kings have always worn their crowns under divine protest, and ever will, "until the thrones shall be cast down." Until this set time in the march of Providence, those nations so ruled, will continue to be enslaved, in a greater or less degree, because they know not the truth as to the rights of government and of the governed. The truth alone will make them free. Then the masses of the people will arise in their majesty, and their *will expressed* will be sovereign law. Then royal error, hoary with age, will topple to the ground. And the people will be free. Then the old tyrannical dogma—the divine right of kings—shall find a grave from which there will be no resurrection. Republicanism, or the ancient of days, as great High Priest, will perform the obsequies, without a tear: while the peoples and nations will chant the chorus—"The truth hath made us free."

CHAPTER X.

"THE WAITING ISLES,"

Or our County Described by the Prophet.—Isaiah lx.

THE Land and the Church in ancient Israel are always connected. The Holy Land was God's gift to His holy people, for their possession, in order to their development. This they held by a divine title, until their mission was completed—until their "first principles" and typical condition were finished. Then they were scattered to the ends of the earth, at the time when "the daily sacrifice was taken away." They had acted and finished their part in the great drama of theological instruction. But when Israel is restored, it must be, according to the prophets, on a grander scale than ever before. Ancient Israel was but one family, settled in a very small and limited territory: but Israel restored is to be gathered from all nations

160

and languages, and is to be set up in a vastly
larger territory. Israel restored is to have
the headship of the world, in the work of
reformation, in civil and religious liberty, in
overthrowing all despotism, in purifying the
currents of social life, by a general diffusion
of the religion of Jesus Christ which will then
be felt to be the salt of the earth and the light
of the world. Ancient Israel furnished the
world with the Bible, and with the only plan
of salvation. Israel restored is its expounder
and exemplification, to show to the nations
and peoples its heavenly teachings by which
man may be freed from the bondage of sin, from
the bondage of superstition, and from all sorts
of slavery. It is to show to the world man's
highest status attainable under the Gospel,
both as to Church and State, and that form of
government best suited for human development and religious prosperity. Truly, a
glorious mission !

It is this land of prophecy and providence,
this land of the restoration, which Isaiah saw
and describes so glowingly in this chapter.
As he looked across the ages and saw that
country which the Lord had kept hid for His

people until the appointed time, with the glory of the Lord shining upon it, he bursts out with a grand shout of admiration and wonder at what he saw, saying:

V. 1. "Arise! be light, for thy light is come and the glory of Jehovah has risen upon thee."

V. 2. "For behold, the darkness shall cover the earth and a gloom the nations, *but* upon thee shall Jehovah rise as the sun and his glory upon thee shall be seen." The "but" in this verse is the proper translation, for the Hebrew *vav* is put before *adversative* clauses, and means "and yet"—"but"— "since." The antithesis lies in the thought, rather than in the *vav*, as in Gen. ii: 16, 17, "of every tree of the garden thou mayest freely eat, *but* of the tree of the knowledge of good and evil, thou shalt not eat of it." Also Gen. xvii: 21, xlii: 10.

"The darkness shall cover the earth," means the darkness of sin, the darkness of the fall that put everything out of joint, both civil and religious.

"And a gloom the nations." They had some idea of religion and some notions about

human government; but nothing was clear.
It was all foggy, cloudy and indistinct—more
dark than light, more wrong than right. This
was the gloomy pall that covered the nations.

"But upon thee," upon Israel restored,
"shall Jehovah rise and his glory upon thee
shall be seen." The Sun of Righteousness will
dispel the darkness which had settled down
upon the Church and dimmed its light. He
will give new life and new light: new life to
the Church in her great mission of salvation
and redemption; and new light to the government of the nations. Indeed, upon Israel
restored, Jehovah shall rise as the sun, and
scatter rays of light, "and his glory shall be
seen upon thee." Then the Church shall
"look forth as the morning, fair as the moon,
clear as the sun, and terrible as an army with
banners."

V. 3. "And nations shall walk in thy light✓
and kings in the brightness of thy rising."
This translation is approved by the highest
critical authorities, and expresses exactly the
mission of the fifth nationality. Its clearer
and purer light will have a transforming
influence upon the nations, so that they shall

walk in its light. Their entire organization,
social, religious and civil, will be so changed
as to conform to Israel restored. It will be followed as the highest and best form of human
government. This seems to be the meaning
of the prophet, for he says, "Nations shall
walk in thy light," or follow thy example.

V. 4. "Lift up thine eyes round about [*i. e.*,
in all directions] and see; all of them are
gathered together; they come to thee; thy
sons from far off shall come and thy daughters
at thy side shall be supported." The prophet
looks round about in every direction among
the nations of earth, and he beholds the people gathered together as if in consultation
concerning that wonderful country where a
great light is shining and where the glory of
God is seen, in the extent of the land, in the
freedom and prosperity of the people, and in
the liberty and triumphs of the Church.
Their minds are made up. They are determined to go. "They come to thee; thy sons
from far off shall come." And then the prophet
adds another thing of astonishing interest
that he had not seen among the nations—
"Thy daughters shall be supported at the

side." "Daughters," is in apposition with "sons." The "sons" are the men of the land and the "daughters" are the women. That old interpretation which represents the daughters or the women as infants, carried on the sides or in the arms of men is false, and not consistent with the prophecy, or with the glory of that country described. I think the prophet saw the men of that country in all the dignity of manhood and the women supported at their side, that is as equals in society, as helps meet for them, and companions in life. "Thy daughters shall be supported at the side"—not at "the head," to rule over men, as some fanatically contend; nor at "the feet," to be tramped upon, as in many heathen countries—but supported at "the side" as equals, as companions, to be cherished and loved. The prophet saw woman's true position and remarked upon it, as one of the attractive features of that country, that was to have an elevating and purifying influence upon the nations of earth.

V. 5. "In that place, thou shalt see and rejoice, and thy heart shall throb and be enlarged, because the abundance of the sea shall be turned upon thee; a host [nations] shall come to thee."

Az is a demonstrative particle, originally of place, and means here "in that place," in the land of Israel restored, thy heart shall throb with joy because of great prosperity. "The abundance of the sea," or the wealth of commerce, "shall be turned upon thee." This land with the Atlantic on the east, the Pacific on the west, the Gulf on the south, and the great lakes on the north, furnishes ample room for the commerce of the world. Moreover, "a host, [nations] shall come unto thee." Even now more than a thousand immigrants daily come to our shores. How accurately the prophet has described this land!

V. 6. "Abundance of camels shall cover thee; young camels of Midian and Ephah; all of them from Sheba shall come; gold and frankincense shall they bear and the praises of Jehovah as good news."

V. 7. "All the flocks of Kedar shall be gathered for thee; the rams of Nebaioth shall minister to thee; they shall ascend with good-will my altar, and my house of beauty I will beautify." This is a political description of great commercial prosperity. The terms and names used are oriental, but deeply impress us with the idea of the wealth and piety of the land and people described. With all the cargoes of earthly products, they also bear the praises of Jehovah as good news wherever they go. Their flocks and herds, sources of wealth, minister unto the Lord. "And my house of beauty I will beautify." May not this all beautifully describe the vast physical resources of our country with its commerce and manufactures, with its untold agricultural wealth, and flocks and herds counted by millions? May not these make up the ornaments with which the house of the Lord, or the land of Israel, is to be beautified and made attractive in the eyes of the nations? And when, through the "good news" of the Gospel, "Holiness to the Lord" shall be written on all our pursuits, the beauty of His house or land will be complete.

V. 8. "Who are these that fly as a cloud and as doves to their windows?" The prophet looks again, while the panoramic vision is passing and beholds ships of commerce and transportation with outspread sails like fleecy clouds, coming in multitudes to our shores. He must have seen our country at the time we are now living, and further on, when immigrants and trade are coming from every land. The evident meaning of the prophet is that the people were coming here to the land he saw in vast multitudes to live and traffic.

V. 9. " Surely the isles " [or distant lands beyond the sea, or maritime regions very remote] " shall wait for me and ships of Tarshish [or Spain] foremost [or first] to cause to come in thy sons from far off [countries] their silver and their gold with them, for the name of Jehovah thy God, and for the Holy One of Israel, because He has honored thee."

Diodorus Siculus, an ancient historian who lived about the time of Cæsar Augustus, says the term, "isles," in his day, meant "undiscovered lands supposed to lie in the Atlantic Ocean." This also accords with the Hebrew word [eyyem] "isles" which means distant lands beyond the sea. In this verse we have a sublime announcement of our great country, definitely pointed out. " Surely the isles shall wait for me." The undiscovered lands of America were lying hid for thousands of

years, far off in the uncrossed Atlantic. It
was waiting the set time in God's purpose
and providence. It was waiting for monarchy
and despotism to act their part and show
what they could do, or rather to show what
they could not do, to elevate and amel-
iorate the condition of men. They had a fair
chance, and a long time to bring forth ripened
fruit, but behold, sour grapes. Their effort
was a failure, and worse than a failure. Hence
they are to be broken to pieces and driven
away like chaff before the wind. "The isles
were waiting" for every form of autocracy to
show its utter insufficiency to work out man's
highest political destiny. They were waiting
till the Reformation would give the human
mind a new impetus and broader views. They
were waiting until the great principle of self-
government should move the masses to seek a
new theatre, in which to realize the blessings
of popular freedom. They were waiting for
the leaven of the Gospel to do its great preparatory work, for the printing press to dif-
fuse general intelligence and thus educate a
people intellectually and morally, until well
fitted to set up an enlightened republican

government. The isles were waiting till the set time to favor Zion should come.

"And the ships of Tarshish [or old Spain] foremost [or first] to cause to come in thy sons from far off" [countries]. This prophecy has been literally fulfilled. Did not the ships of Spain first discover this country and open the way for immigration to the new world? After Columbus had been repulsed from every court in Europe, did not Ferdinand and Isabella lend him the necessary aid, and America was discovered? This was the divine programme, revealed 2,500 years ago. It was enacted in the right time and by the divinely appointed parties. It is passing strange that the world of Bible readers have not recognized this great prophecy and its fulfillment long ago! This prophecy cannot refer simply to the spread of the Gospel, for missionaries are *sent out* to the heathen; but here the sons of God are represented as being *brought in* from different and distant homes to a newly dis-covered country. This prophecy cannot refer to Judea, for it was not then an undiscovered country. And the ships of Spain never could bring the first inhabitants to Palestine, because that old country was inhabited before Spain was born. Hence the utter unfitness of all these interpretations.

"Their silver and their gold with them." They came with the intention of making this land their home. They brought their treasure with them. But why did they come? This is an interesting question. The prophet answers it. "For the name of Jehovah thy God, and for the Holy One of Israel." Our sainted ancestors were persecuted for their religion. Because they dared to worship God according to their convictions of truth, they were driven out and found homes in the New World. They came here "for the name of Jehovah their God." When the Portuguese came—when Pizarro and Cortez and the minions of monarchy came to America, they came for gold, and took possession in the name of their respective governments. But when the Huguenots, the Quakers, the Puritans and the Covenanters came, they came for conscience's sake and "for the name of the Holy one of Israel." And when they took possession of this land it was not in the name of an earthly sovereign, but "for the name of Jehovah their God, and for the Holy One of Israel."

> " Not as the conquerors came,
>   They the true-hearted came :
>   Not with the roll of the stirring drum,
>   Or the trumpet that sings of fame.

> " Ah, call it holy ground,
>   The spot where first they trod :
>   They've left unstained what there they found,
>   Freedom to worship God."

" Because He has honored thee ": this seems to be the grand reason why He has so dealt with " the waiting Isles." He has honored thee in making thy land the scene of Israel's restoration. He has honored thee with that government, symbolized by the " Stone," which crushed monarchy and drove it from the earth. He has honored thee as the agent whose mission is to bless the nations with civil and religious liberty. Ten thousand blessings are thine, " because He has honored thee."

V. 10. " And strangers shall build thy walls, and their kings shall minister unto thee ; for in my anger I smote thee, and in my favor I had compassion on thee."

The prophet continues his address to the land saying, "strangers shall build thy walls." The white man was a stranger in the first settlement of this country. He was so called and considered by the Aborigines; and more forcefully still, he felt himself to be a stranger in a strange land and surrounded by a strange people. Hence they began to build "walls" or forts or fortifications for their safety, to defend themselves against the sudden and bloody attacks of surrounding savages.

"And their kings [the kings of these strangers] shall minister unto thee." The kings of Europe ministered unto this land by sending out colonies and sustaining them in their feebleness; by encouraging emigration; by granting charters; by establishing governments; and in various ways "the kings" of these strangers ministered unto the settlement and development of the land.

"For in my anger I smote thee." During uncounted centuries the land was occupied by savages. All its greatness amounted to nothing. It brought forth no ripe fruit. Its desolation amid such magnificence showed that its God in anger had smitten it. But now how changed the scene! Civilization and the gospel have come to give life to the dead—life to the dead resources of the land, and life to the hearts of the people. Now, the praises of the Holy One of Israel are echoed from the mountains and the plains, while the busy hum of millions tells of a prosperous and happy people. God's anger is exchanged for love. Of a truth "In my favor I had compassion on thee."

V. 11. "And thy gates shall be open continually; day and night they shall not be shut, to cause to come in unto thee a host [nations], and their kings drive them off."

The prophet looked forward 2,500 years and saw things just as they now are and have been. "And thy gates shall be open continually" means the sea-ports of our country are open to the ships of all nations, to bring in, not only their articles of commerce, but emigrants seeking homes in a more congenial clime, where their prospects are brighter, and life may be made more desirable. The "nations" have heard of this land and its "open gates," and they are coming in "hosts." The boundless prairies and the open country of the West invite them to come, and they are coming by thousands and tens of thousands. These arguments are causing to come unto thee "a host," yea, even "nations."

"And their kings drive them off," by tyranny, by oppression and by persecution. How, many thousands in the early settlement of our country came hither for conscience's sake. They were not allowed to worship God as they pleased, and they chose expatriation rather than religious servitude. "Their kings" stirred up their nests in their fatherland, and "drove them off." By the Revocation of the Edict of Nantes, 500,000 Huguenots left France for foreign countries, and many of them came to our shores. Protestants were excluded from office and places of trust. If they were not married in the Catholic Church, their marriage was illegal and their children were called bastards. Not only in France, but in other kingdoms, by wars and bloody persecutions and annoyances of less magnitude, "their kings drove them off." And multitudes of them directed their way to this land of "open gates," where liberty may be enjoyed to the full. And they have come

and are now coming by "hosts" and by
"nations." In the single State of Texas, the
Bible is published and sold in thirteen different languages. And the cry is, still they
come at the rate of a thousand a day. A feel-
ing of unrest among the nations is a bountiful
source that keeps the stream of emigration
flowing with an increasing swell upon these
shores. The high claims of monarchy and
autocracy will always be a disturbing element, to drive off their people to that country
where the highest offices may be obtained and
filled by men from the humblest walks of
society; where *true merit alone* is, or ought
to be, the badge of promotion.

V. 12. "For the nation and the kingdom
that will not do work for thee shall be destroyed; yea, those nations shall be utterly
desolated."

This is what the prophet saw after looking
down the track of our history. He has simply
recorded great facts that he has witnessed.
"The nation and the kingdom that will not
do work for thee," *i. e.*, co-operate with thee
in the work of civil and religious liberty, in
promoting human freedom, spiritual freedom,

mental freedom, and the gospel of salvation,
and in exalting Christ as King of nations—
all those nations which oppose the progress
of the march of truth, "shall be destroyed,
yea, those nations shall be utterly desolated."
This is the grand mission of the Stone government, as revealed by Daniel, to crush
and destroy all forms of absolutism, and
to establish in their place free governments,
in which Christ alone is King. "For the nation and the kingdom that will not do work for
thee," in scattering seeds of truth, in diffusing
light among the masses, in promoting popular
freedom, in elevating man to his highest temporal condition, and in giving free course to
the Gospel to accomplish its holy mission,
"shall be destroyed; yea, those nations shall
be utterly desolated."

V. 13. "The glory of Lebanon shall come
to thee; the pine, the hard oak, and the
box together, to adorn the place of my
sanctuary; and the place of my feet I
will adorn." As the cedars of Lebanon
helped to adorn Solomon's temple and Jerusalem, the place of His sanctuary, so in this
great land of Israel restored, we have vast

forests of pine and cedar, and hard oak and cypress, and all sorts of timber, for groves and ornamentation. Thousands of fine churches, adorned with pine, and hard oak, and cedar, and cypress, all over the land, beautify the place of my sanctuary. "The place of my feet I will adorn": the whole country, the place of His feet, is being rapidly adorned with residences, academies, towns, cities, and adornments of all kinds made from the rich profusion of building material. Truly, "the place of my feet I will adorn." The huts and cabins of primitive life, have been substituted by a vastly improved architecture.

V. 14. "The sons of thy oppressors, [or those who afflicted thee,] shall come bending to thee, and shall bow themselves down to the soles of thy feet; all those who despised thee; and they shall call thee the city of Jehovah, Zion, the holy of Israel."

Has it not already come to pass that the sons of those who oppressed and afflicted us, yea, the descendants of the very soldiery that murdered our citizens, burned our towns, and distressed our people, have come by thousands, to submit to that government which they at-

tempted to destroy? Yea, they acknowledge
its success, and cringingly beg for office, or
places of profit. They have come and cast
in their lot with us; have invested their
wealth under the protection of the government they tried to crush. They now honor
the experiment of human freedom they once
despised. They scoffingly said our boasted
independence would be buried with Washington. But now they are willing to venture
their all under the protection of that flag they
sneeringly said would be the winding-sheet
of American liberty. God's ways are higher
than man's ways, and His thoughts than our
thoughts.

Truly, "there is a divinity that shapes our
ends." This Stone government is His own
providential establishment. Even those who
once despised our political experiment now
acknowledge its power, and behold with astonishment the grandeur of its success.

"They shall call thee the *city of Jehovah*,"
so manifest are His dealings with us. In
fact, He is our great Governor, and exercises
executive authority in the affairs of the nation. "Zion, the holy of Israel" shalt thou

be called; that is, this people and land will be sacred to Him, for it is the home of millions of God's people, and it is the grand centre from whence pure rays of light, from the sun of civil and religious liberty, are going out, and will go out, with increasing brightness, to bless the nations of earth with new life, and a higher development, spiritually, politically, and in all the departments of human progress. This is the divine mission of the "Stone,"—also of " the ancient of days,"—of " the Man-Child,"—of "Israel set up the second time."

V. 15. "Instead of being ruins, and ugly, and none passed through, I will make thee a perpetual excellency, a joy from age to age."

This is a cheering statement. Our country lay in ruins for thousands of years, unimproved and ugly; and none passed through; no commerce with the nations, no one to beautify its mountains, or cultivate its plains. The whole land lay in rubbish and ruins, undiscovered and unknown to Japheth, the leader of the world. Instead of this desolation and neglect, "I will make thee a perpetual excellency from age to age." Here, the Gospel is preached. Here no mitered priest or kingly crown directs the affairs of Church or State. Here, every man is free to vote or worship as he pleases. Our simple system of republican self-government gives the largest range to human capability. A man's own will and capacity alone limit his attainments. He may reach high, and obtain all the wealth and position he can. This is every man's right and privilege, and none dare rob him of it. The Constitution and laws of the country protect him in every honorable and praiseworthy avocation. Here, every man is a king, and his house is his palace; he bows only to sovereign law, for the public good. Verily, the Lord hath made this land "a perpetual excellency." And when He tells us it shall be "a joy from age to age," it should inspire us as a people, and especially all our law-makers and rulers with a holy zeal and a deep devotion, to accomplish its grand mission among the nations. For this government is to continue "from age to age." It will steadily improve in morals and manners, as it grows in years. Its legislation will be purged and purified. Whatever is rotten in the body-politic will slough off, as having no sympathy or vital connection with its vital growth. Our legislators will gradually improve in moral courage, so that *golden arguments* will have no power to turn them from the way of right. Then the cess-pools of iniquity and vice, which are now a stench in the nation, will be removed or dried up and cleansed, because no longer protected by law. Then a purified and healthful atmosphere will minister to a healthful growth and to a vigorous and virtuous development. This is not a fanciful forecasting, but directly in accordance with the teaching of the prophets For this government is not to share the fate of other governments that have preceded it. The history of its rise and progress will be written, but never that of its fall. It will be more and more perfectly developed, until it rests under the bright light of millennial glory. To this end, may the Lord rule among our rulers, and "teach our senators wisdom."

V. 16. "And thou shalt suck the milk of nations, [*i. e.*, get their wealth] and the breast of kings thou shalt suck, and thou shalt know that I, Jehovah, am thy Savior, and thy Redeemer, the Mighty One of Jacob."

The prophet here tells how this land of
Israel will grow in wealth and power. Sucking is a drawing process to obtain the milk.
So the attractions of this country have drawn
hither the milk of the nations. And in the
early settlement of our country, when the
Huguenots, the Quakers, the Puritans, the
Covenanters, the Scotch and the Scotch-Irish
came, we not only sucked the milk of nations,
but we got the cream—the very class of men
our country needed, who were trained in the
school of Providence and best fitted for laying
the broad foundation of this great government. And since then, millions of brawny
arms have come, and are still coming, to develop the limitless resources of the land, to
cultivate the soil, to open the mines, to build
our railroads, even from ocean to ocean.
Truly " thou hast sucked the milk of the
nations."

"And thou shalt suck the breast of kings."
Some of our learned commentators seem to
think this clause is a catachresis—a rhetorical
blunder—where the sense overleaps the style.
But not so. God makes no blunders, rhetorical, or other; but commentators often do,

when they don't know what they are wri-
ting about. This prophecy means just what
it says. For just in proportion as we " suck
the milk of the nations " and absorb their
wealth and power, in the same proportion we
increase our own wealth and greatness. This
sucking of the milk of the nations comes first,
by which we are made more powerful and the
better able to " suck the breasts of kings,"
i. e., take from them their tyrannical power
and iron rule, and suck from them the starch
out of their stiffening, and make them more
like other men—suck from their autocratic
domination, and take from them the power to
persecute the Church, to shed innocent blood,
and to trample God's people under their feet.
So wonderful shall be the growth of this
country in wealth, in power, in true religion,
and general intelligence! And its reflex influence on kings shall be so amazing in soften-
ing, moderating, and changing their rule, and
compelling them to regard the rights of their
subjects, that " thou shalt know that I, Jehovah, am thy Savior, and thy Redeemer, the
Mighty One of Jacob." Men shall see and
know that such mighty results are brought

about by the hand of God, and not merely by human wisdom. His hand is and has been so manifest in the affairs of this country, that even the wicked see it and profanely say, " there is a strange providence that takes care of children, negroes, and the United States."

V. 17. "Instead of the brass, I will bring gold; and instead of the iron, I will bring silver; and instead of the wood, brass; and instead of the stones, iron ; and I will make thy officers peace, and thy rulers justice."

Israel restored, is here described as being vastly richer than ancient Israel. The contrast is minutely made. The Hebrew definite article expresses it. " Instead of *the* brass of ancient Israel, I will bring gold to Israel restored; and instead of the iron, I will bring silver ; instead of the wood, brass ; instead of the stone, iron. The difference between the two estates is not in *kind*, but in *degree*. In the first estate Israel was confined to one family ; in the second, Israel is to bless all the families of earth. If it took all the silver and gold mentioned concerning ancient Israel, to meet her demands, it will now, in the dispensation of the Spirit, in the world-wide work,

take millions more. If it took one-tenth of
the income of every man in ancient Israel to
support the Tabernacle, what will it take now
to support the Gospel, and to send its heavenly
news to the ends of the earth? The Lord has
given us a land equal to the tax, and with that
tax paid promptly, He guarantees unfailing
prosperity. With increased responsibility He
has increased our resources. During the first
300 years after America was discovered, it
furnished 3½ time more gold and 12 times
more silver than all the world besides. Our
hills are burdened with iron, more than enough
to build a network of highways from ocean
to ocean, and our ships and palaces. Our
resources are absolutely inexhaustible.

"I will make thy officers peace and thy
rulers justice." We have no knighted herald-
ry, no pomp and power of privileged classes
to trample on the rights of the people. All
our "officers are peace." No military trap-
pings to tyrannize over us, but every man is
peaceably tried by his peers. "I will make
thy rulers justice." Our Constitution requires
the laws to be executed with justice. Frequently justice is robbed of its aim, not be-

cause of defect in organic law, but because of
human corruption, incident to fallen man. The
civil code of the States is based on the principles of eternal right. So that it is true ours
are "officers of peace and rulers of justice."

V. 18. "Violence shall be heard no more in
thy land, desolation and ruin within thy borders, and thou shalt call thy walls Deliverance
and thy gates Praise."

For long centuries the Church had a baptism
of blood. Violence seemed to be her heir-
loom, handed down from age to age. "I came
not to send peace, but a sword" has been
fearfully realized. The names of Smithfield,
Piedmont, St. Bartholomew, Inquisition and a
score of others will tell to the latest generation
of the violence endured by the Church. But,
thank God, there is now a land where violence
shall be heard no more. Desolated homes
and ruined fortunes for Christ's sake shall
never be seen within thy borders. "Thou
shalt call thy walls Deliverance and thy gates
Praise." Here the Lord's people are delivered
from the blood-hounds of cruelty. They are
free and safe, forever safe, and "thy gates
shall be praise."

V. 19. "Thy sun shall not be to thee any more for a light by day, and for brightness the moon shall not shine to thee ; but Jehovah shall become thy everlasting light, and thy God thy glory."

In this verse we have another of those adversative clauses where *vav* is translated "but." The people of God for many centuries had been driven from country to country by terrible persecution. They had been hiding in dens and caves of the mountains. Their life had been made a living death. For hundreds of years the Claverhouses of Satan had turned loose their hellhounds on the track of Christians. But, in the good providence of God, a country was discovered in which the Stone Kingdom was set up—where Israel should be restored. The persecuted ones see it, and come by thousands and scores of thousands. Here, they are free to worship God as they please, free from oppression and from persecution. In this land "violence shall no more be heard." They are so happy that the light of the sun by day and the moon by night is considered no light at all in comparison with the goodness of God experienced by them and their great joy of heart, "for Jehovah shall be thy everlasting light and thy God thy glory." The Sun of Righteousness shone upon them so brightly, so cheeringly, that the shining of the sun and moon are nothing to be compared to their spiritual illumination, to their apprehension of the goodness of God in giving them *peace*, glorious peace, peace that flows like a river. Truly "their God was their glory."

V. 20. "Thy sun shall go down no more, and thy moon shall not be taken away, for Jehovah shall be to thee for an everlasting light, and the days of thy mourning shall be ended."

The sun is a symbol of civil government. See Isa. xiii : 10 ; xxiv : 23 ; Jer. xv : 9 ; Ezek. xxxii : 7. Joel ii : 31 ; Amos viii : 9. "Thy sun shall go down no more," as in ancient Israel. That people accomplished their mission, and were scattered among the nations. Their government was utterly destroyed. Their political sun went down in blood, and their people became exiles and fugitives. But in Israel restored, thy sun, *i. e.*, thy civil government, shall go down no more. "I will make thee a perpetual excellency, a joy from age to age."

"Thy moon shall not be taken away." The moon is a symbol of the Church. Ancient Israel rejected the Savior. "He came unto His own, and His own received Him not," therefore they were cast off. "The daily sacrifice was taken away," and their government and Church went down: but in Israel restored, their civil and religious privileges and blessings shall continue forever; her "moon shall not be taken away; for Jehovah shall be to thee for an everlasting light, and the days of thy mourning shall be ended." The Church is no more to take refuge in the wilderness; racks, stakes and gibbets are no more to be the death places of the saints. These horrid monuments of torture crowd the pages of the past; but now, let all praise to Jehovah's name be given, because "the days of thy mourning are ended."

V. 21. "And thy people all of them just [*i. e.* doing and loving justice] shall possess the land forever, the sprout of my planting, the work of my hands, to glorify myself."

To the just and upright man the Hebrews
attributed also *kindness* and *liberality*. See
Ps. xxxvii : 21; Prov. xii : 10; xxi : 26. This
then being the meaning of the word "*just*"
in this connection, it gives an exact description of the people of our country. Their kindness of disposition, and liberality to all, are
notable characteristics of American citizens.

"Shall possess the land forever." It will
not be given to other peoples. Great changes
may take place, and must take place. Great
progress and improvements in every department will be made; but the government will
always remain an elective, representative
government. For all of monarchy is to be
utterly destroyed; because kings have always
worn, and now wear, their crowns under the
divine protest; and when autocracy is swept
away, there will be no other form of government left to manage or control the masses
of mankind, except representative republicanism.

"The sprout of my planting, the work of
my hands." These are love-words which the
Lord hath spoken to His people. They contain
a soul-cheering promise of perpetual posses-

sion ; His people " shall possess the land forever." This country is the sprout of His planting, the work of His hands to glorify Himself." By this we understand the providential settlement of God's people in this country, under a form of government divinely approved, under the government of "the sprout of Jesse "; where Church and State are mutually dependent for the progress and prosperity of the whole. The Church cannot do without the State, and the State cannot do without the Church ; while they are separate, and each independent, their prosperous and harmonious co-operation plainly shows that this country, so pointedly described by the prophets, is the " sprout of the Lord's planting, the work of His hands."

"To glorify myself." Where the great principles of truth and righteousness are culti- vated, where the divine law is respected and honored, where light and liberty are diffused among the nations, where love to God and be- nevolence to our fellow-men abide, there truly the Lord is glorified in His wonderful love to the children of men, nationally, socially and ecclesiastically.

V. 22. "A small number shall become a thousand, and a few in number shall become a mighty nation. I, the Lord, will hasten it in its time." Our country in its beginning was "a little one," but now it has become a mighty nation. And yet, it has only commenced its growth. Truly the Lord is with us. He is marshaling His forces for grander conquests. For He has said, "I, the Lord, will hasten it in its time."

CHAPTER XI.

"BEHOLD I DO A NEW THING,"

Or the Primal Curse Rolling Back.—*Isaiah xliii. 18-21.*

18. "Remember not former things, and things of old shall not be rebuilt." As if the prophet had said, ' Why should I refer to ancient instances of God's almighty intervention in behalf of His people, when others quite as remarkable are to come? Remember not the former condition of ancient Israel. Set not your heart upon the land of Judea, nor think to restore it to its former glory.' It had served its purpose in the economy of grace; it had been the cradle of the Church; it was well suited for its home in infancy; its territory was admirably adapted in all respects in which to accomplish its divine mission. But now the Church is "God's warrior " to conquer the world, and it must have another land, more accessible,

194

vastly larger and better fitted every way to
be the headquarters of the Lord's conquering
host.

"Old things," or the former estate of the
Church, "shall not be rebuilt." This is a
positive statement that ought for ever to set
at rest that false interpretation which says,
"Israel restored" means that old Judea is to
be re-inhabited, and all the tribes of Israel
must return to Palestine, the temple must be
rebuilt, and I know not what other things are to
be done; this interpretation is all gratuitous
and as fanciful as it is false. This theory is not
consistent with the teaching of God's word,
nor with the glorious development of the
Church "in the latter days." For the prophet expressly says the "old things," or things
of old "shall not be rebuilt." This is an
astonishing statement, nevertheless it is true,
because the Lord hath declared it. The word
translated "rebuilt" is the hithpael of the
verb *banah* "to build." I cannot see how it
can be consistently translated "consider,"
and thereby change the whole meaning of the
verse. That translation, or rather that substi-
tution, is without foundation—without a cor-

responding word in the original and entirely gratuitous. It brings to this passage a cloud of smoke instead of a flood of light. This word, *banah*, is one of the great decisive words in the Bible which must be translated correctly. Gesenius gives the meaning of this word " to build " in all its forms but never to " consider." The commentators are as silent as the grave on this word. They did not know what to do with it and retain their notions about the restoration of Israel in old Palestine. This whole passage is irreconcilable with that old theory and declares directly against it.

V. 19. "Behold I do a new thing. At this time it shall spring forth ; shall ye not know it, [or shall ye know what it is] ? I will even place in the wilderness a way [or a going] and streams in the waste place."

"Behold I do a new thing," for the Church and for my people. Something that the world had never seen before—something on a grander scale than were the former things and the things of old, so great that the former things will not be remembered.

"At this time it shall spring forth," at the

time when "I do a new thing." All this implies that this "new thing" was far in the
future, or at least not then developed.

"Shall ye not know it, [or do you not know
what it is]?" This seems to be a divine chal-
lenge for inquiry and investigation.

"I will even place in the wilderness a way
[or a going], and streams in the waste place."
This is the answer to the question just asked.
This is the "new thing" I will place in the
wilderness, in this country that had been
"always waste," in that "land shadowed
with wings," in the land of Israel restored,
in our own America—"the wilderness," "a
way," or "a going," I will build. The form
of this expression is singular, but the sense
is collective, doubtless referring to the great
system of railways that now form a net-work
of "goings" to and fro: the highways on
which millions travel. And was it not in this
country that steam was first successfully applied to navigation? This interpretation is
confirmed by the next expression, "and
streams in the waste place." What sort of
streams? Does it not mean the vast current,
or streams of population now flowing into our

country, that was for thousands of years a
wilderness and a waste place. Our country at
present furnishes a literal, a wonderful fulfillment of this prophecy. Truly it is "a new
thing" that has come to pass, a new country
and a new people, gathered from all lands, by
a new mode of transportation and locomotion ;
such as the ancients never saw. Ancient Israel had its day, and did its preparatory
work : and now the Lord is doing "a new
thing" in Israel restored ; in comparison
with which former things shall "not be remembered." The setting up of the Stone kingdom
marks a new era in the world's history, civilly,
socially, religiously, and mechanically. Small
sailing vessels and old time wagons and ox
teams are now substituted by floating palaces
and lightning express trains. That was a slow
age of plodding—this is the steam age of
locomotion. This makes a new page in history and a new epoch in the world. Truly,
this is a new thing the Lord hath done. As
" the glory of the latter house shall be greater
than the former," so Israel restored shall be
greater than ancient Israel. The next verse
also confirms this interpretation.

V. 20. "The living thing of the country ✓ shall honor me, the great serpent and the daughters of shouting, because I have placed waters in the wilderness, streams in the waste place, for the watering of [or refreshment of] my people—my chosen."

What is "the living thing of the country?" It is something that has power and motion. It passed in vision before the prophet, unlike anything he had ever seen before. He had no name for it. He saw its extended and varied operations, and its wonderful doings. Hence he called it "the living thing of the country." It is all clear to us; we meet it in our every day experience. It is so common that it has almost lost its novelty, but none of its truthfulness, as a great realization. It is the application of *steam* to *machinery.* ✓ This unseen, mighty power turns our mills, rolls the wheels of commerce, prints our papers, furnishes employment for millions. It comes on a mission of mercy to oxen, horses, and men, and relieves them of the hard bondage of burden-bearers; it takes their place in locomotion and transportation. In thousands of ways, it honors the Lord, in the development of the "wilderness" which He gave to His people in making it beautiful and to blossom like the rose. One illustrious example, showing how it honors the Lord, is in the buildings of the American Bible Society. It strikes off the Word of God with almost incredible rapidity, and that, too, in many different languages, and scatters it broadcast over the world. Thus in many ways "the living thing of the country" honors the Lord.

"The great serpent, and the daughters of shouting." This is a graphic description, but not more graphic than true, of a long railroad train, drawn by a hissing, snorting locomotive: as it glides along, bending with the curves of the road, it looks to a distant spectator like a great serpent, bent on some mission of terror. In our thoroughfares of trade, and great manufacturing centres, the perpetual noise of screaming and yelling engines forcefully remind us of the prophet's description, "daughters of shouting": they, too, are honoring Him, and shout His praise in various ways, by developing the resources of His land, and building up His people in power. The words translated, "daughters of shouting" have been translated "jackals, or wolves," also "owls, and ostriches." There is some reason for this last translation, for the word (*yaha-nah*) that means an ostrich, is identical with the word in the text, that is derived from the word (*hanah*) "to cry out," "to shout." The learned expositors came very near the meaning, without reaching it. The prophet is here describing something that he had never seen or heard before, by things and terms that were familiar and best suited to convey his meaning. Dr. Livingstone, the great explorer of Africa, says he never could distinguish at a distance, the roaring of an ostrich from the roaring of a lion, only by this fact, the ostrich roars in the day, and the lion roars at night. This explanation satisfactorily fixes and defines the prophetic description of "the living thing of the country" and "the daughters of shouting" to mean locomotives, and various noisy steam powers, as you will see presently.

"Because I have placed waters in the waste places." "Waters," in the Scriptures, is often used as a metaphor, to represent multitudes of people. So we think here it aptly represents the vast population that is flowing, and will continue to flow, into our great country; which was so long a "waste place."

"Streams in the wilderness." It is not (*nharim*) streams, currents, floods of water, but (*nharoth*) with a feminine termination, signifying streams of various sorts—streams of population, streams of wealth, streams of learning, and streams of influences that will make glad the city of our God, "for the watering, or refreshment of my people —my chosen." Notice the vast preparation He has made for His people, for His chosen: that their temporal wants may be abundantly supplied, that His chosen may lay aside forever their soiled and tattered garments of exile and imprisonment, and that their souls may be refreshed with the waters of life, that they may honor Him in the salvation of men, and also in the liberation and elevation of the nations.

V. 21. "This people I have formed for myself; they shall declare my praise."

√ "This people," formed for the great work of glorifying God, in the development of civil and religious liberty, for the utter overthrow,

and entire destruction of despotism, and political slavery, for the promotion of human
freedom among the peoples, for the elevation
of the oppressed millions of earth to a higher
social, civil and moral status.

"They shall declare my praise." This is
their mission—to declare the praise and glory
of their great Master, both at home and
abroad, until the ends of the earth shall unite
in ascribing "Blessing, and honor and glory
and power, unto Him that sitteth upon the
throne, and unto the Lamb forever and ever."
This seems clearly to be the meaning of this
prophecy. This is the *new thing* that the
Lord of Hosts would do. He would restore
Israel to nationality "the second time," to
great honor and worldly power in that "far-
off" land, that had "always been waste:"
and through its influence revolutionize the
nations; throw them out of the old ruts of autocracy and non-progress, and give to the
tribes and peoples liberty of thought, liberty
of speech, and liberty to worship God according to the dictates of their conscience.

It is certainly no "*new thing*" for wolves
to howl, for ostriches to run or roar, nor for

owls to hoot, as some have interpreted a part of this prophecy. Neither would it be a *new thing* for rivers of waters to flow through the wilderness, where they had been flowing for thousands of years. There is no "new thing" about this; and yet the Lord declares, "I will do a new thing," and He meant what He said, and He has done it. He has done a new thing on a grand scale, in the establishment of the fifth nationality, in the setting up of the Stone Kingdom, in setting up Israel the second time in this "far-off" land, that He kept hid for ages. "This people have I formed for myself; they shall declare my praise," in a manner never done before. Through them, in a great measure, He has rolled back the curse of Eden. "The living thing of the country" is honoring Him in a thousand ways that cannot here be recounted; but especially does the "living thing" furnish to the people astonishingly rapid and easy locomotion. Instead of men and women plodding on foot over long and wearisome journeys, as in times of old, we can accomplish pleasantly in a few hours what once required weeks and months. Instead of the old

stage-coach, we now have express trains drawn
by " the living thing of the country," to carry
the mail and passengers. But greater yet, the
telegraph carries a message around the world
in a moment of time. This work of praise has
just begun; astonishing things in every department have been accomplished, and vastly
greater triumphs are just ahead, now laughed
at by fools, but soon to be sublimely realized.
In the agricultural department of "toil and
sweat," with the present improved implements
one or two men can do more than a dozen in
times of old. Once Ruth, Naomi and a number of others toiled for days in the burning
sun of summer to reap and bind the wheat in
the fields of Boaz. Now women are spared
that pain. Two or three men with a reaper
and binder drawn by horses or by " the living
thing of the country " can accomplish in a few
hours what once took all the men and women
on the plantation weeks to do. Once Dorcas
had to toil with her needle all day, and far
into the "wee sma' hours of the night,"
straining her eyes by the dim light of a tallow
candle; now she can do ten times more work,
and ten times more pleasantly, with a sewing-

machine by the bright sunlight, and read or rest at night as she may please.

Thus in numberless ways in these " latter days " God has given freedom from the drudgery of toil. Behold in these and other blessings the primal curse rolling back, as the light of the gospel advances, as liberty is given to the mind and men, as the Church rises upon a higher and wider plane.

These are some of the " new things " which the Lord said He would do, which He has done and is now doing, for that people whom He has formed for Himself, that they might more gloriously " declare His praise."

CHAPTER XII.

THE STONE KINGDOM A POLITICAL POWER.

"SHALL NEVER DESTROY ITSELF."

Confirmed by One of the Endings of the "Forty-Two Months," which Points with *Exactness* to May 26, 1865, when the Last of the *Confederate Forces were Surrendered.*

DAN. ii : 44. "And in the days of these kings [*i. e.*, these ten-toe kings] shall the God of heaven set up a kingdom, which shall never destroy itself (*hithpael*), and the kingdom shall not be left to other people, but it shall break in pieces and bring to an end all these kingdoms, and it shall stand through the ages."

Daniel is the only one of all the prophets who has given us a chronological view of the rise and fall of the great world-powers from his day to the end of time. He was prime minister in two of these—in the Babylonian and Medo-Persian. His position through a long and changeful life eminently fitted him,

207

both as a man and a prophet, to map out the great political powers that should succeed each other. It is true the Church was connected in some way with all these successive kingdoms, as the great centre of attraction and observation. Daniel saw her oppressed, wronged, martyred, exiled and suffering unrighteously under all these political dominations, until the Stone Kingdom, or fifth government, was set up. He sympathized with the Church; his heart yearned for her, but yet you can see the influence of his life-long education as a statesman in the prominence he gives to political matters. How minutely he traces the rise and fall of kingdoms with chronological accuracy and has mapped the nations, is demonstrated by subsequent history. The Babylonian, the Medo-Persian, the Macedonian and the Roman empires have all passed away, and the ten-toe kingdoms have been standing for a thousand years.

"And in the days of these [ten-toe] kings shall the God of heaven set up a kingdom that shall never destroy itself." This last verb is not passive but in the *hithpael* and means "shall never destroy itself." All the

preceding kingdoms had destroyed themselves
by their own weakness and wickedness, but
this fifth nationality, he foresaw, would not ⌄
share the fate of its predecessors. The great
colossus with its golden head, with its arms
and breast of silver, with its belly and thighs
of brass, with its legs of iron, and with its feet
and toes of iron and clay, Daniel interprets
to be different political governments, and the
history of the world confirms the truthfulness
of his interpretation. So also the stone cut ✓
out of the mountain without hands must sym-
bolize a political government different from
all the rest as stone is different from metal.
This must be the true interpretation, for it is
to crush and to destroy with great political
and military power all these other kingdoms.
It is to be hurled against them like a tornado
with the destructiveness and enginery of battle till they be driven away from the earth
like chaff from the summer threshing-floors.
This clothes the Stone with terrible military ✓
and political power. Again, since Daniel gave
a view of all the great political powers from
his day to the end of time, and since the
Stone, the last in the series, has a revolution-

izing, overthrowing and destroying power, it
must also be political in its organization.

" This great image whose brightness was
excellent and the form thereof was terrible,"
was metallic and represented all of monarchy
and autocracy that would ever exist on the
earth. The Stone was constituted of an entirely different mineral and symbolized an entirely different kind of government, as has been
shown.   It symbolizes a government of representative republicanism.   Also the time of its
rise " in the days of these [ten-toe] kings " is
specially mentioned and corresponds exactly
with the setting up of the United States. Also
this wonderful providential government which
was cut out of the mountain of Christianity.
that the God of nations hath Himself " set
up," is astonishingly demonstrated to be the
United States by its corresponding history.

The next great truth to which special attention is invited, is that the Stone government
" shall never destroy itself, and the kingdom
shall not be left to other people." This is
different from all other kingdoms and governments.   They have risen, have flourished
awhile, and have fallen, and have been left to

other people. There is no exception to this
universal rule found in the history of the ages.
All the nations of the past, like men, have had
"a time to be born and a time to die:" not so
with the Stone Kingdom. It had a time to be
born specially marked and pointed to, and it
was born on the exact day and year foretold
by the prophets : but it is to have no end, as
other nations have ended ; "it shall never be
destroyed." Ancient Israel destroyed itself
by wickedness, by secession and division, and
passed away when its work was accomplished, but Israel restored must enlarge and expand until all the nations have been brought
under its benign influence. Its march is ever
onward and upward. Its mission, through the
gospel, is to give civil and religious liberty
to the nations and freedom to the peoples,
also truth and light for superstition and spiritual darkness. The Stone Kingdom is the
United States, and as its course, as marked
out by the prophets, is ever in the ascendant,
reaching on from conquest to conquest, not so
much with garments rolled in blood as with
the olive-branch of peace bestowing upon the
nations liberty, happiness and truth, we can-

not detect in its course with the largest prophetic glasses any declination.

"But the saints of the Most High shall take the kingdom and possess the kingdom forever, even for ever and ever." This much we know, the Stone Kingdom "shall never destroy itself" by secession. That terrible experiment has been made at a loss of a million of men, according to the estimates of Horace Greeley and Alexander Stephens, and eight thousand millions of dollars. And, as a dying soldier asked at the first great battle of Manassas, "What was all this for?" We forbear to answer. But we know it is written in God's eternal plan that this Stone government "shall never destroy itself, and the kingdom shall not be left to other people." Our country needs to be cleansed and purged of much indwelling wickedness and corruption, both political and civil; it must be done, and will be done, however drastic the medicine. But woe to the man, or to the party, that attempts its destruction, or wars against the perpetuity of this government: terrible remedies may be necessary for its purification and healthfulness, but never an effort for its destruction;

such will be warring against the providence of God, and that providence will be too strong for them. Let us see what emphasis facts and figures can give to these Scripture truths about the perpetuity of the Stone government.

We have shown in a former chapter that " from the taking away of the daily sacrifice," to the setting up of this government, was exactly 1,260 symbolic years. This is an indisputable identification. We have shown in another place, from the flight of the woman into the wilderness, " where she is nourished for a time, times, and an half," that her wilderness sojourn began on the 17th June A. D. 325, and ended after 1,260 symbolic days, on July 4, 1776. This is another indisputable identification.

The 42 months that the holy city shall be trodden under foot, is an expression of " the time, times, and an half." It must be remembered that all these periods have several different endings, pointing to different great events. We now desire to call attention to one of the endings, or rather to one of the fingers of the 42 months that points to one of

the greatest events in our political history—
to the close of the war between the States—to
the last surrender; when the Stone with all
its parts was united again.   Let us count and
see whither the divine index points.   By adding Sabbath-day time, to 42 months, or $\frac{1}{6}$,
we have 49—then add other sacred time of
3 months, and we have 52 months—corresponding to the 52 weeks in a year.   These
52 months have 30 days each, making 1,560.
Now 70 weeks—the key to all these " times "
and " years "—or, 490 divided into 1,560 gives
us $3\frac{9}{49}$.   A Hebrew year of years is 364 multiplied by 364,—equal to 132,496: add to this $\frac{1}{7}$
for Sabbatic time, then add to that result $\frac{1}{6}$ for
Sabbath-day time, and we have 176,661$\frac{1}{3}$.   This
is one symbolic " time "—then multiply this
" time " by $3\frac{9}{49}$, and we have 562,432 days.
This reduced gives 1,539 years and 324 days.
The student must remember that the Julian
Calendar, which is still in use in the Russian
Empire, and was in use in all Europe until
1582, makes the civil year 11 minutes longer
than the solar year, which now amounts to
about 12 days too much, and must be sub-
tracted from the previous result, which leaves

in solar time 1,539 years and 312 days; or, in months, it will be November 9. A fraction of a day is counted a whole day. The reader will remember that A. D. 325, June 17, was the day when Church and State were united, was the time when the woman fled into the wilderness, and the time from which these 42 symbolic months, or 1,260 days are counted. The reader will also remember that the first ending of these 42 months, has been shown in a previous chapter to be on July 4, 1776, the birthday of our nation; and the second ending points to some other great event, further on, in our national history. Now to A. D. 325, June 17, add 1,539 years and 312 days, or November 9, and we have exactly A. D. 1865, May 26. This is the second ending of these 42 months, and points to the second great event in the history of the Stone kingdom—to the very year and day, when Gen. E. Kirby Smith surrendered the last of the Confederate forces to Gen. R. S. Canby, of the Federal army. On that day the Stone was no longer divided; on that day prophecy had a wonderful fulfillment; and the truthfulness of the divine programme was confirmed before the eyes of the nations. These figures are startling, and the facts revealed are astonishingly sublime. This great colossus of prophecy stands in the dignity and eloquence of silence, with eyes fixed, looking across the ages, and with his arm outstretched, and his finger pointing to May 26, A. D. 1865, and yet he speaks not a word, but with a look of warning and reproof, he reminds us of what had been spoken ages since, the government "shall never destroy itself, the kingdom shall not be left to other people." Thus these figures and facts have given a powerful emphasis to the truthfulness of God's word, which declares that the Stone kingdom "SHALL NEVER DESTROY ITSELF."

CHAPTER XIII.

OUR COUNTRY AFTER THE PROPHETIC PATTERN.

And What our Rulers Ought to Do.

"FOR thus saith the Lord God, Behold I, even I, will both search my sheep, and seek them out as a shepherd seeketh out his flock in the day that he is among his sheep that are scattered; so will I seek out my sheep, and deliver them out of all places where they have been scattered. in the cloudy and dark day. And I will bring them out from the people, and gather them from the countries, and will bring them to their *own land*, and feed them upon the mountains of Israel, by the rivers, and in all the inhabited places of the country." This is their *own land* that the Lord had "kept hid" through the ages, so that, "in the latter days" He should "set them up a second time," or restore His Israel, in the fifth nationality, for

217

the conquest of the world for King Jesus. "I
will feed them in a good pasture, and upon
the high mountains shall their fold be: there
shall they lie in a good fold, and in a fat pasture
shall they feed upon the mountains of Israel.
I will feed my flock, and I will cause them to
lie down, saith the Lord God." Ezek. xxxiv:
24; xxxvii: 21; xxxviii: 8.

In this little volume I have called attention to a few of those marked and wonderful
prophecies that point to and describe our
country, as the land of Israel's restoration;
to those prophecies that have been fulfilled,
or are now being fulfilled, with astonishing
accuracy; and to those prophecies that never
can have their fulfillment in any other land on
earth; for no other land corresponds so perfectly with the prophetic description as this,
even as the shadow fits the substance. The
time of the rise of our country coincides exactly with the time mentioned by Daniel and
John. Its geography, boundary and division
into thirteen States, at its birth, coincide exactly with the description given by Ezekiel.
The direction of this promised land, from old

Palestine, lies exactly in the course pointed out by Isaiah. And the land he described as " shadowing with wings," and having a people, when discovered, that were " tall and naked, and terrible from their beginning, and far away," coincides exactly with the geography and aboriginal history of the two Americas. Here in this land of the Stone, a multitude of prophecies have a perfect fulfillment. Even to enumerate them would be tedious, and to re-capitulate, would be like telling the story over. There are scores of other prophecies that relate to this country, many of which have been fulfilled; and many that are exceedingly glorious, point to periods further on in our history; but as they belong to the future, we say nothing about them: their exposition will be given in God's own time. We have endeavored to write about *facts* and only those prophecies that have been realized, so that, in contending for the truthfulness of our expositions, we would be able to point to the prophecy as the shadow, and to our country as its substance, and show their divine fitness, their perfect coincidence, and, of course, perfect fulfillment. When the reader has finished these pages, I protest against his saying, "it is an ingenious work," because such a criticism doubts the truthfulness of God's word, and the wonderfulness of His providence. When the Lord has declared a series of prophecies, extending through thousands of years, and then, in His own time, and by His own providence, fulfills these prophecies, and when a servant shows their fulfillment to his countrymen, should that exposition be called ingenious? Should we not rather admire the wonderful works of God, whose sleepless providence fills the eternal programme minutely, even from the falling of a sparrow to the rising and falling of kingdoms and nations, exactly in their appointed times; that our faith may be strengthened, and our hearts encouraged. We must throw our prejudice to the winds, and bow before the God of truth, however astonishing His truth may be, or however wonderful His ways. "Let God be true, though every man be a liar."

Since this is the land where Israel is " set up the second time," and since the evidence of this great fact is so manifold and indisputable, it behooves the people of God, who are Israelites indeed, to "arise and build the walls" of the spiritual Jerusalem; for Sanballat, Tobiah and Geshem are here, with all their forces, to oppose and hinder the work. Let every man of Israel, who is "a soldier of God," gird on the sword of the Spirit; yea, let him put on the whole armor of the Gospel, and go forth to the conflict, "for the work is great." Infidelity, false philosophy, and all sorts of error must be overthrown. Millions among us need "the washing of regeneration, and the renewing of the Holy Ghost." The time has come when truth and righteousness should unfurl their banner on all the high places of our country. The destiny of the world is placed in our hands, according to the divine programme. Then let the light of truth, religious and political, shine forth with increasing brightness on this generation and upon those that follow.

I hope it will not be considered impertinent or presumptuous to speak a word to the rulers of our country; to all those who are "in authority," from the highest to the lowest; to all who have charge of the affairs of government. The long looked-for "Stone has been cut out of the mountain without hands." "The ancient of days" has come, and its political authority has been restored on a vastly larger scale. These graphic symbols of the fifth nationality, are, and are yet further to be, realized in the United States. This government is to expand in territory and to develop in power, until its glorious mission has been fully accomplished. We will not dwell upon that part which is not yet realized; it has been minutely delineated by the prophets; and God's providence will fit the substance to the shadow, "in its time." This great prophetic country is yours—God has given it to you; and you are its rulers. It is your province to make its laws, and it is yours to execute them. More than twenty centuries are looking down upon you, with unabated interest, to see into what manner of people and government you will be developed. And as yours is, and is to be, the highest type of national development the world has ever had, or ever will have, your every step in the march of progress will be closely scrutinized by the nations. Hence it behooves you to cling to eternal justice and right; justice in legis-

lation, and righteousness in the execution of
law, as the sheet-anchor of your safety. Then
will "mercy and truth meet together, righteousness and peace will kiss each other."
There are certain great wrongs that demand
righting by your hands, as rulers in the Stone
government.

1st. *Great crimes* too often go *unpunished*,
especially where gold is the defense of the
criminal. This is a great wrong to the State
and to society, for it is a license to crime ; its
tendency is to lawlessness and bloody revolution. The only remedy to secure an absolutely impartial and righteous administration
of law, is for the people to return to the ancient custom of electing all judges for life,
or during good behavior ; and require merit
alone to be the elective qualification. Then
the argument of votes can have no weight in
the decision of causes, or power to pervert
justice. When great crimes go unpunished,
and the people submit to these wrongs without
protest, they thereby become *particeps criminis.* Then the whole community, or State,
thus sympathizing with crime, becomes ripe
for pestilence, famine, or some terrible pun-

ishment, as a righteous visitation of providence.

2nd. *The Sabbath law is too seldom en-
forced.* This is a great wrong to the State.
The God of law reserved the Sabbath for
Himself, and the man who appropriates that
holy day to his unholy purposes is guilty of
robbery. If a man plows on the Sabbath day
he is liable to be indicted: but a hundred railroad trains may go thundering along on the
Sabbath, and disturb religious worship, and
destroy the quiet and peace of the holy day.
And besides all this these thoroughfares of
traffic and travel keep one million of men from
going to church on the Sabbath by their ceaseless occupation, and thereby damage the
morals of the country ; and yet these railroad
magnates and officials are not indicted for
their accumulated violation of law. Also the
country through which these Sabbath-break-
ing railroads run, by submitting to, and aid-
ing and abetting in this wrong, become *parti
ceps criminis.* All those countries that have
despised and desecrated the Sabbath, have
sooner or later brought upon themselves the
curse of heaven, as the history of ancient Is-

rael and other nations abundantly testifies.
The Lord will not allow His Sabbaths to be
trampled upon with impunity. Works of necessity and mercy are all right; but the constant violation of ·the Sabbath is all wrong.
And since this is to be the great model
country for the nations, our rulers should
rectify this wrong before some terrible curse
befalls us. For the Lord of the Sabbath is
the God of all forces, and He will punish
guilty nations, as well as guilty men, for the
willful violation of His law.

3rd. The general Government and State authorities *license the manufacture and promiscuous sale of intoxicating liquors.*

This is a great national wrong, authorized
by law. A horrible sin against heaven and
humanity legalized. The drink-shops all over
the land are the altars to Baal, which Jeroboam hath set up to turn away the heart of
Israel from the service of the Lord of Hosts.
And the 600,000 drunkards in our land, are
finished jobs, out on exhibition. About 75,000
die annually, and go out in disgrace. But the
recruits are more than the slain. Think of
the oaths and blasphemies and profane bab-

blings that ascend from these altars of Baal,
like the smoke of the bottomless pit: also
think of the wail of woe constantly ascending
from countless widows and orphans and
desolated homes. But I will not enlarge.
The evil is enormous, and on the increase. It
not only destroys the soul, but it damages
society, and the best interests of the State.
Also the rulers of the country should remember that they are shaping a government that
is to be a pattern for all the nations of the
earth, sooner or later. This is the divine programme of the Stone, the great Christian republican government that is " to fill the whole
earth," This then being the heaven-appointed
mission of our nation, it behooves our rulers
to right these great wrongs which bring and
will bring a blasting and a curse upon our
people. The Congress of the United States
have the interest and well-being of this nation
in their hands, and whatever opposes its well-
being should be removed. The promiscuous
sale of intoxicating liquors is opposed to the
well-being of our country—it is an immeasur-
able curse, and ought to be removed. This
can be most effectively done by congressional

legislation; by prohibiting the manufacture and sale of distilled, intoxicating liquors in the United States. Then make the violation of this law a felony; because it involves the life and happiness of millions. The good people of the land will sustain such a law, and demand its enforcement. These are some of the many wrongs that your superior wisdom must grapple with and remove. The *rulers* of all countries have great responsibilities, but yours are vastly greater, because of the part you play in the drama of nations, and because of your matchless destiny, as written by the prophets. Therefore " Be strong and quit yourselves like men," " and keep the charge of the Lord thy God, to walk in His ways, to keep His statutes and His commandments." "And who knoweth whether thou art come to the kingdom, for such a time as this." "That search may be made in the book of the records " of the nations, and they " shall tell thee what thou oughtest to do."

A word of exhortation to the citizens of our country may here be in order. Since the whole is made up of all its parts, and since each citizen forms a part of the Stone king-

dom, and must assist in giving it its fore-
ordained impetus, in order to accomplish its
great mission: and since your lot has fallen
in Israel Restored, in the fifth nationality, that
should arise " in the latter days," spoken of
by the prophets, upon whom the eyes of the
world are now turned, " what manner of per-
sons ought ye to be in all holy conversation
and godliness." It is yours to beget and
cherish a sound and virtuous public sentiment
on all matters of government and social life.
For the government of the Stone is of the
people, and proceeds from the people, and
since a stream cannot rise higher than its
source, it is necessary that the people be
truthful and virtuous; then their rulers will be
compelled to reflect their sentiments, by the
enactment of virtuous laws; then our statute
books will be pure and white, a bright reflec-
tion of righteousness, justice and truth. How
glorious will be that end—and it will certainly
be attained—in comparison with the statute-
books of to-day, whose leaves are pure and
white indeed, except here and there are pages
as black as hell, while others are of a darkish
gray, on which are written legal compromises

with sin. While necessity, dressed in the livery of heaven, stands with saintly bearing, and pleads the part of, and offers excuses for legalized crime, these black pages must be washed and made white and clean, and the people alone can have it done. And, thank God, from the signs of the times, the washing day is near at hand when it will be done. Already the people are groaning under a burden of wrong—physical and moral wrongs— and are longing to have all their laws the counterpart of eternal truth and right. Your statutes, like common law, should be the expression of justice and righteousness, and when they are less than this, the people are *particeps criminis*, and are guilty of the crimes legalized. But as light and truth become brighter and purer among the people by increased intelligence, legislation will be correspondingly improved. Therefore trim the lamps of learning, and "let there be light," both to head and heart. The necessity for a steady growth, for constant development and improvement in all things, social and civil, is manifest from your divinely-marked destiny: for your country must have the headship of the world, *i. e.*, it must give to the nations a model government, where the people shall be free, and Christ alone shall be king. Not only will this country have such a government, and offer such for adoption to the nations, that they may enjoy civil and religious liberty to the full, but it will compel the nations to adopt a representative republican government, by the power of moral suasion, or otherwise; for " the Stone must fill the whole earth." In confirmation of this great truth, we know from the signs of the times, and from God's revealed plan of procedure, that monarchy shall be driven away from the world, " and no place will be found for it." This then being your high destiny, it becomes the duty of each and every citizen to perform faithfully the work assigned him, socially, politically and religiously. A strange and wonderful providence has presided over the birth, and directed the amazing developments of our country up to the present moment. And we are assured that the same providence will direct the affairs of our country " through the ages," and all along their widening and ascending scale, to the exact and glorious fulfillment of the Stone's wonderful mission. And now may the citizens of these United States realize that they are indeed " that happy people whose God is the Lord," and direct their steps accordingly. To this " let all the people say,

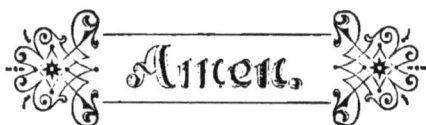

Amen.

www.ingramcontent.com/pod-product-compliance
Lightning Source LLC
Chambersburg PA
CBHW030317270326
41926CB00010B/1397